ORDINARY PEOPLE, *EXTRAORDINARY TIMES*

ADVANCE PRAISE FOR
ORDINARY PEOPLE, EXTRAORDINARY TIMES

"Every generation is asked to defend what the last one fought for—and to push further. For decades I have watched ordinary people do extraordinary things when they believe their actions matter. Skye Perryman has written exactly the book this moment demands, and she's written it for all of us."

—*Dolores Huerta,*
labor leader and civil rights activist

"*Ordinary People, Extraordinary Times* is a clarion call for everyone ready to meet this national and global crisis—and win. Skye Perryman deftly weaves history, anecdote, and proof of concept into a refreshingly accessible work that leaves no one behind. Like her Herculean efforts to hold our courts to their purpose, Skye's book does the same for Americans and our democracy. A must-read and must-do."

—*Stacey Abrams*

"These are troubling times for our democracy—but Skye Perryman has provided a manual for people who are tired of wringing their hands and are ready to roll up their sleeves. *Ordinary People, Extraordinary Times* is a practical guide to policy and action from a leader who has spent years on the front lines of the fight and knows how change actually gets made."

—*Hillary Rodham Clinton*

"Skye Perryman's seminal book reminds us that lawyers, lobbyists, pundits, and political operatives will not save our democracy. Only we, the people, can do that. Perryman steps up to the plate and provides a path for how ordinary people can move from spectator to change agent while finding agency, fulfillment, and even joy. Written by one of the leading forces opposing authoritarianism, this book is a road map out of the political wilderness in which we find ourselves. A must-read for every civically minded individual."

—*Anthony D. Romero,*
executive director, ACLU

"There are moments in history when sitting on the sidelines stops being an option. Skye Perryman knows we're in one of them—and she refuses to let any of us pretend otherwise. *Ordinary People, Extraordinary Times* is the rare book that captures why this moment is so urgent—and then hands you something to do about it."

–Reshma Saujani,
New York Times bestselling author of *Pay Up*
and founder of Girls Who Code

"Justice at the top depends on what we do every day at the bottom. Skye Perryman's *Ordinary People, Extraordinary Times* will help to restore the power of every reader."

–Gloria Steinem,
writer and activist

"Skye Perryman understands that getting our country back on track will take all of us, and she's providing the tools we need to meet this moment. *Ordinary People, Extraordinary Times* is an inspiring and empowering guide for every American who wants to see our nation thrive as a beacon of freedom and democracy."

–Governor JB Pritzker

"When people say we are living through extraordinary times they surely aren't kidding, but we are here and for a reason. We just may be the ones we've been waiting for. Let's find out together. Skye Perryman offers a glimpse of a world most thinking people are ready for, and she offers not more angst and the obvious, but real direction."

–Annie and Willie Nelson

"A lot of Americans have stopped believing anyone in Washington is actually listening. I get it. But Skye Perryman isn't asking you to trust the machine—she's asking you to understand it well enough to show up and fix it. This book is for all of us, regardless of your politics."

–Michael Steele,
former chairman of the
Republican National Committee

ORDINARY PEOPLE, *EXTRAORDINARY TIMES*

A GUIDE FOR ALL OF US

How to Reclaim Your Power, Fight for Freedom, and Reimagine Democracy

Skye Perryman

PRESIDENT & CEO OF DEMOCRACY FORWARD

TEN SPEED PRESS

California | New York

TEN SPEED PRESS
An imprint of the Crown Publishing Group
A division of Penguin Random House LLC
1745 Broadway
New York, NY 10019
tenspeed.com
penguinrandomhouse.com

A Ten Speed Press Trade Paperback Original

Typefaces: Bitstream's Century Schoolbook, Linotype's Futura, and Monotype's Sabon

Library of Congress Cataloging-in-Publication Data has been applied for.

ISBN 979-8-217-27399-7
Ebook ISBN 979-8-217-27400-0

Editor: Thea Diklich-Newell | Production editor: Terry Deal
Designer: Aubrey Khan | Art director: Emma Campion | Production designer: Mari Gill
Production: Dan Myers
Copy editor: David Robinson | Proofreaders: Tracy Rothschild Lynch, Miriam Taveras
Publicist: Kate Tyler | Marketer: Chloe Aryeh

Manufactured in the United States of America

1st Printing

First Paperback Edition

Cover design: Isabelle Gioffredi

The authorized representative in the EU for product safety and compliance is Penguin Random House Ireland, Morrison Chambers, 32 Nassau Street, Dublin D02 YH68, Ireland, https://eu-contact.penguin.ie.

FOR RENICK

and all our children who will inherit

the country we leave them

A portion of the proceeds from this book will support the work of Democracy Forward and Democracy Forward Foundation.

Power concedes nothing without a demand. It never did and it never will. Find out just what any people will quietly submit to and you have found out the exact measure of injustice and wrong which will be imposed upon them, and these will continue till they are resisted with either words or blows, or with both. The limits of tyrants are prescribed by the endurance of those whom they oppress.[1]

–Frederick Douglass

There is a mysterious cycle in human events.
To some generations much is given.
Of other generations much is expected.
This generation of Americans has a rendezvous with destiny.[2]

–Franklin Delano Roosevelt

As a first step, we must restore our belief in ourselves. . . . Let each person do his or her part. If one citizen is unwilling to participate, all of us are going to suffer. For the American idea, though it is shared by all of us, is realized in each one of us.[3]

–Barbara Jordan

Contents

Note to the Reader

I KNOW HOW YOU FEEL—because I've been there too.

You stay awake at night, made sick to your stomach by the latest news, when you haven't even had time to digest the horrible events from the day before. Some nights, you may wonder if you are safe. Other nights, you may *know* you are not safe. Either way, you know that when you wake up, something else will have happened, something that, not so long ago, you may never have imagined would take place in your own country. You meet up with friends and ask how they are doing, and they give you that knowing look that says, "*Oh, I'm okay . . . except for the slow-motion train-wreck that may end the American democratic experiment.*" You laugh weakly because you understand exactly what they are saying—that the political back-and-forth and ability to agree to disagree that many have relied on in our democracy has become broken. That norms have been not just crossed but trampled. And while everyone sees it . . . no one can seem to align on how to pull us back from the brink. On a good day, the country is only back-sliding slowly. On a bad day, and there are many bad days, our nation's backslide from democracy into autocracy accelerates.

Untrained, masked federal agents are running roughshod in our streets, terrorizing communities. Peaceful protesters have been killed. The government has been weaponized, and the Supreme Court feels stacked. It is harder and harder for many to make ends meet. Even working people cannot afford housing and to put food on the table. The social safety nets have eroded. The wealth we generate for the companies we work for doesn't come back to us; instead, it gets funneled into the pockets of a few who are enabling the horrors committed by this government. And a huge media-tech ecosystem feeds us realities that cannot be trusted. It all feels like so much. Like too much.

We are all tired. And many of us are numb. We are losing our ability to sustain outrage at the abuses of power and corruption that confront us every day; incidents that alone would have been Watergate-level scandals decades ago simply slide off the front pages to make room for another abuse or tragedy. It's almost impossible to keep up; even harder to know what to do.

If you are feeling this way—or have loved ones who feel this way—this book is for you. It is for ordinary people living in an extraordinary time. It is about understanding what is happening in our nation and doing something about it. Some of you have been fighting for a long time already, some of you have ancestors who also fought, and some of you are just jumping in. However you come to this time, we need you.

We have to acknowledge that there is no cavalry coming to protect us. No knight in shining armor to save us from the situation we are in. It's up to us. We are the people who decide what happens next. While daunting, it can also be empowering to know how essential we are in the fight for freedom and our democracy.

I mentioned that I've been in your shoes; I've felt lost, afraid, confused—and powerless. But I've learned that we have power in the way we respond to what is happening. Action is an antidote.

This book is about reclaiming our collective power. It is about fostering community, courage, and joy in an unreal time. Here you will find tools that ordinary people have used in extraordinary times before us—actions that if we take together can help us fight for freedom today, build for a better tomorrow, and create extraordinary change.

"Forward"

I BEGAN WRITING THIS BOOK in March of 2025, after the president of the United States invoked the Alien Enemies Act, a wartime authority, to remove people from the country without due process at a time when the nation was not at war. Previously, the Act had only ever been used during the War of 1812, World War I, and World War II. This new shocking move in the dark of night was an escalation not only of the administration's anti-immigration agenda but also its disregard for the Constitution and the rule of law. It was a threat to our basic freedoms as Americans. It was the kind of scary step that transcended traditional politics.

As a lawyer and the president and CEO of Democracy Forward (a nonpartisan, national legal organization that represents people in court and promotes the advancement of democracy), that late Friday evening when it happened is seared in my memory. Our legal team and lawyers at the American Civil Liberties Union (ACLU) reacted quickly to assert the rights of the people as the president invoked the Act to deport those he had calculated would be too politically difficult for anyone to defend: Brown men from Venezuela with tattoos, whom the president claimed were members of a violent gang. Before they could talk with a lawyer or speak up for themselves, they were rushed out of custody and onto planes. They were to be removed from the country and sent to a gulag-like prison in El Salvador. Earlier in the week, the president had announced that the American people would soon wake up to "beautiful" stories in the newspapers about what he had done to protect the nation. *But the president had miscalculated.* He had forgotten that our Constitution doesn't only protect the people he favors. It protects every person within the confines of the United States. No one can be spirited away without their day in court. That is what it means to have the rule of law.

A team of lawyers worked through the night to bring a lawsuit in the early hours of Saturday morning to prevent the removals from taking place. We probably surprised the president's team with our filing in a federal court in Washington, D.C., at 1:15 a.m. on March 15, before the planes had even left the United States. That same day, a federal judge called a hearing and issued an emergency ruling: It ordered the government to turn around the flights that were now carrying away our clients, until the courts could consider if the removals were legal.

The administration took a shocking step: it chose not to follow a direct order issued by the court and refused to turn the planes around. After the flights landed in El Salvador, that country's president posted a video on social media of our clients leaving the plane in handcuffs and being delivered to the notorious prison. Then he tweeted "Oopsie . . . too late" with a news headline about the judge's order. Secretary of State Marco Rubio shockingly retweeted the gloating post.

Just before we and our co-counsel filed the case, some people in Washington's political arena, including both Republicans and Democrats, had privately discouraged us from bringing this lawsuit. They wanted us to wait in the hope that we would find more "sympathetic" clients. They warned us that we'd be walking into a political trap. That public opinion would not side with these men, and the president would have his made-for-television image of tattooed purported gang members being escorted from the country, effectively winning his test case for the unprecedented use of wartime powers during peacetime.

Of course, the problem with this approach is that neither politicians nor political image consultants get to choose who is given constitutional protections. The Constitution is clear: "*No person shall be deprived of life, liberty, or property without due process of law.*" The people the president removed from the country had never been afforded an opportunity to explain themselves or to have their case heard. Were they in gangs? No one had asked them. The president's claimed authority to disappear people without process was a threat to all Americans. Judge J. Harvie Wilkinson III, one of the nation's prominent conservative appellate court judges, would later note of the situation, "The government is asserting a right to stash away residents of this country in foreign prisons without the semblance of due process that is the foundation of our constitutional order . . . This should be shocking not only to judges, but to the intuitive sense of liberty that Americans far removed from courthouses still hold dear."[1]

As lawyers, we knew that getting into court in the middle of the night was the right thing to do. We also knew that the American people, even those who might disagree with us on many things, would believe it was the right thing to do. And, we were right. Within days of filing our lawsuit, outrage toward the Trump administration began to build—especially when they defied and mocked the court order a federal judge issued to pause its actions. Soon stories started pouring out that many of the people removed from the country were not criminals or gang members—they just happened to have brown skin and tattoos. These details demonstrated how reckless and wrong their removal without any form of judicial review truly was. By April, polls confirmed that a majority of people across America, of all backgrounds and political beliefs, disapproved of the president's actions.

People in this country—progressive, liberal, moderate, conservative, apolitical—have a deep disdain for brute abuses of power. We don't like bullies or the rule of kings. If the president can shuffle people onto planes in the dark of night and disappear them to a gulag prison in a foreign country without any process, then none of us are safe. The American people understand that, regardless of how or whether they voted.

DEFENDING PEOPLE AND OUR COUNTRY ON ALL FRONTS

By the time we filed the Alien Enemies Act case, late night legal filings had become commonplace for the team of lawyers at Democracy Forward with whom I have the privilege of working. Just after the 2024 election, then-President-elect Trump had proclaimed that he would govern with "shock and awe," a term used by military leaders in 2003 to describe the intense bombardment of Iraq. In his first months in office, all of us witnessed a flurry of executive orders, and his administration attempted everything from trying to delete the Constitution's birthright citizenship guarantee, to freezing essential services like Meals on Wheels and Head Start, to outlawing words like "equity" and "inclusion," and authorizing unprecedented immigration raids into houses of worship, schools, and hospitals.

By March 2025, our team had already filed dozens of federal court cases on behalf of people and communities that found themselves deprived of basic protections. These included: challenging the president's attempt to freeze federal funds and essential services across the nation; contesting U.S. Immigration and Customs Enforcement's (ICE) operations in houses of worship; questioning Elon Musk's so-called Department of Government Efficiency (DOGE), including DOGE team members' reckless access to the American people's personal data; and opposing attempts to indiscriminately fire civil servants, as well as efforts to deprive the American people of information about their government's actions. Our team regularly stayed up all night, readying ourselves for court the next day, to give people the help they needed and to check an increasingly concerning abuse of presidential power. And yet it seemed that the tools we had to make change were limited. On a good day, Congress, which was controlled by the president's allies, was asleep at the wheel. On a bad day, Congress was aiding the administration's coordinated, sow-chaos-and-fear approach toward autocracy. Midterm elections were then eighteen months away. Public engagement wavered between hopelessness and willful ignorance.

But something happened after we and our co-counsel at the ACLU filed the Alien Enemies Act case that early morning in March. As the news of the president's overreach hit, there was a sea change in public concern. All of a sudden, it wasn't just lawyers who were speaking up in defense of rights. It was people. It was the people's turn. Ordinary people—from all walks of life—started reaching out to us in a cacophony of ringing phones. People were listening to court arguments, reading court orders, and taking note of when these weren't being adhered to. The people didn't approve of what the government was doing.

Due process dates back centuries to before our Constitution was ratified and is central to any understanding of how a civil society functions. Hearing that people were being deprived of their right to have their day in court (at best) or being disappeared (at worst) sent chills down people's spines. This was the kind of thing that happened in earlier times or elsewhere in the world. It was reminiscent of the denial of rights of Indigenous communities in colonial America, the slave patrols of the 1700s and 1800s, of the Nazi regime's actions in Germany in the 1930s, the incarceration of Japanese Americans in the United States in the 1940s (for which all three branches of the U.S. government later apologized), the Argentinean government's actions in the 1970s and 80s, or the kidnapping of people in the dark of night as is occurring in modern-day Russia. It offended people's humanity that in 2025 our government would strip someone of their liberty like that. It went against our deepest democratic principles. People started to wonder what could happen when the branches of the government—the checks and balances we're taught about in school—start to break down. How bad could it get?

The people reaching out to us wanted to know if they would be okay. They wanted to know what was happening in their country. And, more importantly, they wanted to know *what they could do in this moment*. Stay-at-home moms in Texas called to ask how they could help. Dads in California wanted to know what to say to their kids when they asked if they were safe. Small business owners volunteered to hold fundraisers and host community events in places like Kansas and Wisconsin. We heard from college professors, nurses, wage workers, students, retirees, line cooks, artists, people from all walks of life, who had begun taking time out to plan protests and meet ups.

Even people who had been sympathetic to the president and generally approved of his "shake up the system" style were disappointed by his overreach and felt betrayed. "I didn't vote for this," one woman from Ohio exclaimed to me. Erstwhile Trump supporter and podcaster Joe Rogan felt the need to distance himself from the president's aggressive immigration tactics, saying, "We gotta be careful that we don't become monsters."[2]

America had reached a moment that was bound to happen—a moment that transcended traditional politics, where it didn't matter if you saw yourself as liberal or conservative. But, more than that, we had reached a moment where ordinary people—including those who do not follow politics or consider themselves civically active—wanted to know what *they could do* because they saw that doing nothing, or hoping for the best, was no longer an option. The future of democracy was at stake.

"In the United States, there is no king." These are the opening words of a legal complaint filed in federal court by our Democracy Forward team against one of the president's early executive orders in February 2025. We were reiterating the foundational idea that underlies the principles of a democratic republic, that here we have a government of the people, by the people, for the people. That there is no king. Those words were echoed by federal judges across the nation and are now a rallying cry for marches across the nation. The No Kings Day rallies have comprised two of the largest single-day peaceful protests in America's 250-year history, with the rally in October 2025 drawing more than seven million people to 2,700 events in all fifty states, D.C., and cities around the world.

Since that time, countless more people have been sparked into action in response to ruthless ICE raids, the violent deaths of people living in America at the hands of the federal government, and the administration's brazen corruption and self-dealing. Spontaneous marches and peaceful protests filled the streets of Minneapolis when federal agents violently occupied the city. The call for no kings isn't just the stuff of court dockets anymore—it is now the stuff of talk at kitchen counters and among diverse communities. This is where the fight for our freedom lies.

As people across America have mobilized, our team of lawyers hasn't slowed down. We and other legal organizations have been in court nearly every day to defend the American people. We have represented organizations comprising millions of people across the nation who have been eager to go to court to protect their rights and the rights of their fellow Americans. When we hit barriers, including at the Supreme Court, we dust ourselves off and pick back up again the next day. The stakes are too high to be derailed by roadblocks, even powerful ones.

Businesses and institutions that have capitulated, or chosen to stay silent, have disappointed us, and many have faced consequences as people choose to vote with their dollars. But in the rare cases in which powerful institutions have had the courage to stand with their convictions, people have noticed. Unlike those that caved to demands, the law firms that sued to challenge the president's targeting of lawyers have been celebrated—and they have won in court. Costco has become a household favorite for many families because it refused to be bullied out of its commitment to inclusion of all people. Chair of the Federal Reserve Jerome Powell spoke the truth to the American people when the president targeted him. Amid great threat, many schools that receive federal funding have continued holding cultural festivals to highlight the strength of our diversity; libraries and small booksellers have insisted on lending and selling banned books; musicians, artists, and writers have spoken out and supported pro-democracy litigation; and houses of worship have continued to boldly proclaim "All are welcome." It still isn't too late for those powerful institutions sitting on the sidelines to choose the right side of history.

COURAGE HAS BECOME THE NEW CURRENCY.
AND COMMUNITY CREATES THE CONDITIONS FOR COURAGE.

Throughout my life, I have seen what happens when ordinary people muster courage and create change in their communities. As a child in Waco, Texas, I witnessed the power that ordinary people's voices had in opposing attacks on our local public schools, in creating community services for the unhoused, and in protecting veterans from cuts to their services. As a Texan, I have seen people who have differing personal views, ways of socializing, and backgrounds all contribute to a community potluck, build a house for a family in need, or come together to save a community program. I have seen people march together when their values are attacked, including over the past year.

As a lawyer, I have worked on hundreds of cases and initiatives to protect and expand people's rights, following my commitment to our Constitution. Through this work, I have seen the incredible bravery of people from all backgrounds and walks of life who have found the courage to declare when their rights are being violated and when their communities are threatened. People who have been willing to act on that courage by filing lawsuits, publicly protesting, or speaking out in new ways. I have also felt and witnessed the pain and sting of injustice that people and communities experience when the call to courage isn't answered by our neighbors, leaders, or institutions.

I started writing this book when it became undeniably clear, as our history also teaches, that it is not our institutions that will save us—not the courts, not corporate generosity, not the universities, not the media—but *the people*. Our elected leaders are entrusted with power limited by checks and balances, yes, but ultimately and most importantly, by the people. When the rule of law is disregarded or the president seeks to redefine the constitutional bounds of their authority, we must rise up. When actions taken by the president and his allies violate basic human rights and our humanity, we must act. As voting rights are decimated by our highest court, we know it is the people who must act.

The threats to our freedom did not begin on Inauguration Day 2025, but they did begin to rapidly accelerate when the president chose to govern in a manner that is on a collision course with our Constitution. For many in this country, the president's actions pile on to what they already experience in their states and local communities, where politicians have passed a rash of laws to ban books, block healthcare, and stigmatize people who are "othered"—such as young people, immigrants, and LGBTQ people—by those in power.

We are living in a time when those who would threaten our freedom have power and are wielding it. They follow a familiar playbook, one followed by other harmful and, yes, autocratic movements—whether in our nation's era of the Jim Crow South or in Vladimir Putin's Russia, Viktor Orbán's Hungary, or during the fascist movements in 1930s Europe. They seek to polarize people, deprive them of hope, isolate them from their sense of community, and snuff out their belief that they can make a difference. In fact, the greatest tool that anti-democratic actors and abusive governments have is the ability to make people feel powerless.

But there are many things that we can do. We may not be able to fix system-wide institutional failures as individuals, but we can choose to defy expectations. We can learn how to use our voices, to ground ourselves in our values, and to act in ways that our history teaches will enable freedom to ring. We can build community, take care of ourselves and our loved ones, and extend our circle of care to those around us. And, when we do these things, our actions can—and do—lead to big changes.

This book is for people asking *What can I do?* in this extraordinary time in our country, for people who are afraid and uncertain about the present and the future. It is intended to provide strategies for showing up wherever you are with your values, including when there are many competing pressures to silence who you are and what you believe. It invites you to learn more and question more—even when this is hard to do. It invites you to acknowledge the challenges of the moment, and find ways to move forward.

In the chapters that follow, you'll find stories from the fight for freedom in courtrooms and communities as well as lessons learned from those fights. You'll see what ordinary people across the nation are doing and how their actions are making a difference, and, I hope, you may be inspired to do the same. The suggestions in this book encompass social and political issues, but they are also about creating the communities that are essential for us to find courage and the steps we must take to commit to one another. This book is about defying attempts to make us feel isolated and alone—and that make us believe we do not have power. Additionally, the stories in this book show that finding joy amid the bleakness is also a form of fighting for freedom.

This book is organized around seven meaningful action steps that we all can and should take, along with analysis and insights drawn from history and my own work alongside people and communities on the frontlines. Within each action step, you will find checklists and tips for implementing the action step or for understanding relevant concepts. Some actions do not require too much time; others may require longer-term commitments. All are optional, as there is no "one way" to take action. These steps are not intended to exhaust you—instead, they are offered to provide a way to get started, to help us all find how we can uniquely contribute with who we are and what we have.

We all have a role to play in this moment. We don't have to agree with one another on all issues. We don't even have to like one another. We just have to find a way forward together—as people who are committed to building a world that will be better tomorrow than it is today.

Two hundred and fifty years ago, this nation was born out of righteous anger at a king and the promise of a new path forward—one never attempted in the known world—where national identity was formed around a series of shared ideals and commitments. These ideals have been tested since they were written in the Declaration of Independence—as the promises of life, liberty, and the pursuit of happiness have rung hollow for the vast majority of Americans long after they were first made. This journey of American democracy has been one of demanding that words become actions—and that the promises made for *all* really include *all of us*. Since the founding of the nation, the tests of our ideals have led to new structures of government, civil war, and pivotal moments and movements from Lexington & Concord, the Underground Railroad, Gettysburg, and Seneca Falls; to the nation's mass mobilization after Pearl Harbor, the steelworker and mineworker strikes of the 1940s, Bloody Sunday in Selma, Stonewall, the Delano grape strike of the 1960s; and to so many more moments that show the power of ordinary people demanding better—without which our nation's democratic experiment would have ended long ago.

In 1936, as fascism raged in Europe and economic depression

hollowed out the lives of many—including my grandparents and great-grandparents—here at home, President Franklin Delano Roosevelt addressed the American people. He knew that as unemployment and uncertainty soared, there was a corresponding rise in hatred and violence. He feared that the rising fascist movements in Europe would take hold in the United States. Knowing that, as in prior times, it would be the ordinary people of this country who would be key to charting a better path, Roosevelt proclaimed that "this generation of Americans has a rendezvous with destiny."[3] He knew that what happened next was going to be up to the people.

Most of us don't look to make history, but, in extraordinary times, history has a way of finding us. Almost a century later, we are again in a pivotal moment in American life. We, too, have a rendezvous with destiny. My hope is that this book can serve as encouragement to each of us about the difference we can make in this time—and that when we look back on this moment, we will be able to say that we ensured our rendezvous with destiny was one that led to freedom for all of us. That upheld equality and the rule of law. That we will be able to say that when fear was everywhere and our president and his allies sought to create costs to operating with integrity and according to our values, we bore that cost—and we did so together. We found our community, we found our joy, we turned anger and sorrow into action and hurt into change. That from courtrooms, to communities, to kitchen counters, to everywhere in between, we fought for our freedom. And our freedom was won.

Skye

How to Use This Book and OrdinaryPeopleAction.com

THIS IS A BOOK ABOUT ACTION. It is a companion and guide for helping you get involved and make meaning out of this extraordinary time. It is for people who are asking *What can I do?* and who may be feeling afraid and uncertain about the present and the future. It is intended to provide strategies for showing up wherever you are with your values, including when there are many competing pressures to silence who you are and what you believe. It is also intended to challenge you. It invites you to learn more and question more—and to challenge yourself to build community and courage and to find joy, even (and especially) when it is hard.

- **Action.** This book is organized around seven actions we all can and should take.
- **Story & Analysis.** Within each action chapter, you will find a discussion of why the action is important to take, where I share stories and insights from what I have learned working with people and communities on the frontlines, as well as what our history teaches us.

While the book draws upon history, experiences from the frontlines of this moment, and social and political theory to help contextualize what is happening in the United States, it does not (and is not intended to) provide a complete analysis of how we got to this moment. But education is power: Find recommended reading lists for greater context and to dig deeper at this book's companion website (information below).

- **Steps & Options.** Within each action chapter, you will find to-do lists, checklists and tips for implementing the action step or for understanding concepts that are discussed in the chapter. Because our nation's situation is ever-changing and dynamic (and because as the people use their power more, the attacks on people may become greater), many resources and references that can be helpful on your action journey are not included in this book so that they remain up to date. Throughout the chapters, I refer you to a companion website at ordinarypeopleaction.com, where you can find more information. The site is continually updated—and it is open for you to contribute your ideas as well.

While we are living in an uncertain and unsafe time—and this book will provide a clear-eyed view of the threats that we are facing—this book is not intended to scare you. Just the opposite. It is intended to equip you with a little inspiration and a lot of information that can be used to help you find courage and joy and to encourage others to do the same. It is intended to provide you with tools to be a part of a generational fight for freedom that you will be proud to say you joined.

DON'T FORGET THE WEBSITE . . . WHAT IS *ORDINARY PEOPLE ACTION*?

This book's companion site, **ordinarypeopleaction.com**, provides up-to-date resources on ways to plug in, take action, and engage. It also provides current information on how to know and use your rights. Be sure to refer to the website as your action companion, because our work will go beyond the scope of this book. You can join the Ordinary People Action community to engage with others who are doing the same.

ACTION 1

Stop Spiraling and Pick Up a Shovel

"NO, WE AREN'T MOVING TO CANADA." I found myself saying these words in exasperation to a friend who had asked me to lunch out of "concern," given my line of work. The previous weekend, Elon Musk, at the time allied with the president, had tweeted about a court order that our team had won. Unrelenting and escalating online attacks had followed the tweet.

This particular case, as with all our cases, had been filed quickly and out of necessity. Shortly after the inauguration, a White House memo announced that by 5 p.m. the next day the administration would order all government agencies to freeze federal funds to services and programs across the nation. This included meal programs for senior citizens, childcare for youth, and important cancer trials and research. That same day, reports surfaced that Medicaid portals were being closed, and within hours, we began hearing from people around the country who were scared and confused about what would happen if the president's order went into effect. Would they be able to access healthcare? Would Meals on Wheels still operate? What about kids who rely upon Head Start? Or community programs in rural areas where there are no other options for assistance?

The White House's directive threatened red and blue states, big cities and small towns, and everywhere in between, risking the well-being of millions of Americans and likely to fall especially heavily on vulnerable populations. It was deeply unpopular with both those who had voted for the president and those who had not, and it was instilling fear for people's well-being, and, in some cases, their lives. Congress, again, was slow to act. Congressional Republicans were unwilling to call out the White House publicly so soon after the inauguration, although many felt pressure from constituents who were about to have essential services removed. Many Democrats protested, but they were in the minority, and with Republicans in control of all three branches of government, they had limited options.

And so our team at Democracy Forward did what it has done so many times: We went to court to sue the government. We represented nonprofit organizations, small businesses, and public health professionals—groups with different priorities, but all of which were going to see their members and missions affected by a freeze of funds.

The people in these organizations were not politicians, billionaires, or celebrities. They were ordinary people doing their jobs who put themselves in the unwanted spotlight by taking on the administration in a public way, opening themselves up to the tweets and threats from the powerful. But they decided that the cost of not acting, of not going to court, was greater than the cost of challenging the president. They knew that allowing a government to trample on the people it is supposed to serve was too high a price to pay. The lawyers on our team at Democracy Forward who brought the case to court in a matter of hours are humans too.

With determination and will—and caffeine—our team filed the lawsuit the next morning, the day the freeze was set to take place. A hearing was set for later in the day.

And we won.

At the time of writing this book, our court order has stayed in place for many months, keeping federal funds available for essential services and programs, protecting people and communities across the nation. It was that win that caught the attention of Musk, the president, and their allies, who took to social media with threats. And it was those threats that led my friend to be so afraid about what might happen next that she suggested that we consider leaving the country.

Her concern is shared by many of us and for good reason. In the months leading up to this book's publication, the administration has ratcheted up its attacks on our freedom, unleashing brutal ICE raids on our communities and in our schools and sending masked federal agents into the streets of our cities; these agents engage in violence against and even occasionally kill peaceful protesters. There have been relentless efforts to deprive 42 million Americans of supplemental nutritional assistance (SNAP) and to reduce access to health insurance, and countless rash actions by the government that have harmed people by taking away their jobs, discontinuing important community and public programs that threaten their futures. They do not hide their agenda, their targeting and racial profiling of Black and Brown Americans and immigrants, their intent to sow fear in the LGBTQ community by rolling back rights and protections, or their attempts to discredit science and undermine the media.

Fear simmers everywhere. In the city where I raise my young son, the national guard has been deployed, and ICE has been in the streets for months. The idea of moving to Canada or another country is not hyperbole but a talk that many people are having with their loved ones. According to a recent Gallup poll, more than 40 percent of young women between the ages of fifteen and forty-four want to move abroad.[1] Beyond this, many of us wake up every day to the constant deluge of social media posts and news, scared about what's coming next.

Living with the real fear of these threats is not distributed equally. Black and Brown people in the United States have long lived in terror of being arrested, killed, or attacked without cause—for simply existing. The threat is now amplified for immigrant communities as well. With this administration, however, the net of people targeted by the government has been cast more widely, the disregard for the law has grown more blatant, and many more people are feeling afraid. These are unprecedented times. And while where to live is a personal decision for each individual, the vast majority of Americans—hundreds of millions of people in this nation—don't have the resources to uproot themselves and move to Canada or anywhere else. This is our country and we are not going anywhere. We must find a way out of the panic, demoralizing fear, and negative spiraling.

We must, as my grandparents would have said, dig in. We must pick up a shovel and get to work.

My grandparents were ordinary people without fancy degrees or credentials. They grew up in modest circumstances in tiny towns in Texas during the Great Depression and learned to tend farms, grow and fish for their food, and live simple lives. They carried their lessons into their adult lives. As a kid, I spent time with them; I learned from them and their neighbors.

My mother's parents lived on a small farm amid the East Texas pines. On many occasions during my visits with them, something unexpected would happen as we were working on the farm, walking in the woods, or helping with the farmhouse. There would be sudden harsh weather, flash floods, or hailstorms sweeping in unannounced, or a backed-up drain or septic tank causing havoc. My cousins, sister, and I would often panic. We'd be worried about seeds we just planted or an outdoor project that might be ruined or slowed due to the weather, and, as we circled around panicking, often my grandparents would come through. One of them would look at us and, with their Texas drawl, say, "*Kids, stop fretting and pick up a shovel,*" and we'd start working together, digging ourselves out of whatever was happening.

One day, when my grandmother, sister, cousins, and I were walking through the woods, we saw a copperhead snake cross a trail and block our path. As usual, we kids panicked, freezing in our tracks. My grandmother went to get a shovel, came back to the woods, and while we stared at her with confusion, she cut the snake in two, burying its head. She then looked up and said, "When are you going to learn that being scared wasn't going to do anything. The shovel did."

My grandparents were not immune to fear, far from it. They knew well the potential impacts on their lives from grave misfortune, but they understood that panicking was not going to get us out of where we were. We had to calm down and get to work.

My grandparents survived the Great Depression and World War II, and while I don't know for sure what they would say about this moment, I imagine that they'd look anyone who would listen in the eye and say, "***It's time to pick up a shovel.***"

It's time to get to work.

HOW WE GOT HERE

To understand what our work entails and what we can do—to pick up our proverbial shovels—we need a clear grasp of where we are and how we got here; of how democracy should work, at least in theory. And, yes, this will likely lead us to spiral and panic. But an awareness of what brought us to our current moment is part of moving forward.

Democracy is a system of government—a framework—that ensures that the government is controlled by and works for the people. The word "democracy" originates from two words from the 5th century BCE in ancient Greece: demos (*people*) and kratos (*power*). Our nation's Declaration of Independence declared that the power of government must come from the people. Just a little over a decade later, with the adoption of the U.S. Constitution in 1789, the United States became a democratic republic which recognizes that power should derive from the consent of the governed (democracy). Our government operates through elected representatives (a republic) and recognizes some individual rights that a "tyranny of the majority," as philosopher John Stuart Mill would later frame it in his 1859 essay "On Liberty," cannot easily override.[2] In the United States, those rights are spelled out in our Constitution, most notably in the Bill of Rights and later amendments, and in our state constitutions. While there is no uniform definition of a democracy or a democratic republic, essential elements of a democratic republic in the United States include:[3]

- **Voting and elections.** The ability of all people of legal voting age to vote and have their votes counted without intimidation, interference, or threat is essential to a democracy. This includes the peaceful transfer of power after elections and judicial review of elections. It also includes fair representation ensuring that communities and community interests are fairly represented.

- **Personal liberty.** A sphere of personal freedom and liberty—human rights—that all people, regardless of the majority, have. These include freedom of speech, freedom to worship, bodily autonomy, freedom of press, and freedom of assembly.
- **Due process.** Related to personal liberty, due process is foundational. It means that you cannot be deprived of your life, your freedom, or your property without some process, such as the ability to object through a court or administrative system. Due process ensures a king cannot have his guards "seize" you without your day in court. This often includes having access to a lawyer and having your case heard by an impartial third party (often a judge or jury).
- **Rule of law and separation of powers (checks and balances).** The rule of law and separation of powers ensure that there are checks on governmental power. In the United States, checks and balances exist in the federal government, in state governments, and the federal and state systems that provide checks on one another. Each of the three branches of government (judicial, legislative, executive) provide checks.
- **Equality.** Equality recognizes that all are equal in the eyes of the law, and it also recognizes equality of difference and of voice, meaning that difference is a strength, and that each person's voice counts equally. Importantly,

equality includes equality of opportunity and ensures a level playing field. Structural and systemic barriers to opportunity, such as discrimination and bias or massive wealth disparities, violate the core principle of equality.

Dig Deeper

Learn More About the Elements of Democracy

Dig deeper by visiting weholdtruths.org (which you can access through ordinarypeopleaction.com). On the site, you will find explanations of the elements of democracy and how you can take action to advance them.

The history of democracy in the United States has been characterized by attempts to bring about an inclusive democracy, expanding democratic ideals to include everyone rather than only a few. There has been progress over the years, but a true democracy that holds and serves all of us has never been achieved in our nation, and over the past few years we have seen declines in the hard-fought gains collectively won in the past. We dig into this below.

THE BACKSLIDE OF AMERICAN DEMOCRACY

In 2021, the year that violent rioters and insurrectionists sought to disrupt the certification of the 2020 presidential general election ballots by attacking the U.S. Capitol on January 6, the United States was added to a list of globally backsliding democracies by the International Institute for Democracy and Electoral Assistance (IDEA).[4] In its annual report, the organization stated, "The United

States, the bastion of global democracy, fell victim to authoritarian tendencies itself."[5] Backsliding refers to a decline in the quality of civil liberties, rule of law, and democratic institutions.

This designation did not come only because of January 6. Researchers found that the United States had been backsliding for some time—since at least 2019—due to a number of factors: rising misinformation and disinformation, a dysfunctional legislature, election denialism, extremism in some state and local communities (including through voter suppression laws), and the failure of institutions (like Congress and the Supreme Court) to routinely protect the rights of people.[6] A notable trend in 2021 was the decline in an effective legislative branch (Congress), especially the inability of Congress to check the executive branch over the preceding years when President Trump was in office.

The United States has since remained on the list of global backsliders every year.

Also, following January 6, 2021, one hundred of the nation's leading political and social scientists warned of the fragility of the United States's democracy.[7] These scholars attributed the danger faced by our democracy to changes in election laws and voting procedures in certain states under far-right leadership like Texas, Florida, and Arizona, among others. They warned that if Congress did not act to expand voting rights access and protect elections, democracy in the United States would further decline. Congress never acted.

In 2023, thirteen presidential libraries—from President Hoover's to President Obama's (and others, including the Kennedy, Reagan, Clinton, Bush, and Nixon libraries)—compounded the warning calls, stating that democracy in the United States was all too fragile.[8]

By the time of the 2024 election, the question was not whether our democracy was going to rise up and achieve a type of twenty-first-century utopia. Instead, it was whether the nation would elect a leader who could slow the backslide and give the country a chance to restore the pillars of democracy or one who would continue the slide toward authoritarianism.

We know the answer. The backslide has not just persisted: it has accelerated.

It is beyond the scope of this book to analyze the 2024 election. The threats to our freedom predated it, and the work we must do extends well beyond managing the consequences of one election cycle. Yet it is important to understand that many people who voted for Donald Trump, or who did not vote at all in the 2024 election, did not believe they were supporting an accelerated democratic backslide. To be sure, there is a right-wing, nationalist movement in this country that is rabidly anti-democratic and pro-white supremacy, a movement that wants to return the nation to the "old way," when many of us did not have full representation or rights. But that movement is a small number of people. The vast majority of the American people want to live in a democratic republic that is free and where anyone can succeed—in short, they want to live in a thriving democracy.

For the last few decades, the U.S. has been experiencing erosions of our freedom—from the suppression of voting rights and the failures of checks and balances to rising inequality and wealth concentration among the very few.

In this section, I look at some key elements of a democratic society, the ways that democracy has been backsliding, and how the move toward authoritarianism has escalated in the past year—things you may have found yourself spiraling about late at night. I also include some immediate actions and tip sheets.

Spiral #1: Erosion of Voting Rights and Rise in Election Denialism. The ability of people to have the freedom to vote and thereby have a say in their government is the foundation of our democracy and democratic values. Further, while the people's ability to vote is important, voting alone is not sufficient for the exercise of human freedom. When the ability to vote is threatened (or nonexistent), freedom itself is threatened.

For most of our nation's history, voting was restricted to particular classes of people. After the Declaration of Independence was signed in 1776, states adopted constitutions that generally followed from English tradition, which limited the right to vote to white male property owners. (Some states applied religious constraints as well). The U.S. Constitution continued to leave the right to vote up to the states. Following the Civil War and the abolition of slavery, Congress passed and the people ratified the Fifteenth Amendment to the U.S. Constitution, which provides that people cannot be denied the right to vote based on race. Some states, particularly those in the South, vehemently resisted, engaged in violence and terror targeting Black people, and adopted a range of policies such as reading tests, poll taxes, and others ("guess the number of beans in a jar"-type tests) to keep Black and Indigenous people, immigrants, and other groups from voting. This systemic anti-Black discrimination, especially arising in the wake of passage of the Fifteenth Amendment, was known as Jim Crow.

The ratification of the Nineteenth Amendment in the early twentieth century secured women the right to vote—but in practice it was still limited to white women across the South, given Jim Crow laws. At the end of World War II (1945) when Americans (including Black Americans) returned home from fighting for democracy abroad, our system's repression and oppression of Black and other people of color remained undeniably inhumane and hypocritical. Calls for civil rights continued to build, and the civil rights movement galvanized.

What Was Jim Crow

"Jim Crow was the name of the racial caste system which operated primarily, but not exclusively, in southern and border states, between 1877 and the mid-1960s. Jim Crow was more than a series of rigid anti-black laws. It was a way of life. Under Jim Crow, African Americans were relegated to the status of second-class citizens. Jim Crow represented the legitimization of anti-black racism. Many Christian ministers and theologians taught that white people were the Chosen people, black people were cursed to be servants, and God supported racial segregation."

—The Jim Crow Museum: Witness, Understand, Heal[9]

The crown jewel of the civil rights movement is often considered the passage of the Voting Rights Act (VRA) of 1965, signed by President Lyndon B. Johnson with bipartisan support. The VRA provided federal protection and prohibited racial discrimination in voting. It removed the barriers of Jim Crow laws, so that the Fifteenth Amendment's guarantee that voting not be denied based on race would be finally realized. The VRA increased voter participation substantially in the years after its passage and led to concrete positive outcomes—greater public goods, like public education, a more diverse Congressional representation, and more lawmakers who championed civil rights and voting rights. Yet there was backlash from the Southern states that had been at the heart of Jim Crow. This hostility was aided in 2013 by the Supreme Court when, in *Shelby County v. Holder*, in a 5–4 decision written by Chief Justice Roberts, it struck down a key portion of the VRA, finding it "outdated" *because of the success* of the Act in keeping voting districts fair.[10] The Court held that "things have changed dramatically" and a core provision of the VRA that required oversight and clearance of states was no longer needed. Immediately after *Shelby*, Southern states again started to put in place practices that increased the rate of voter registration purges and systematically harmed the ability of people to vote.

Threats to elections and voting intensified after the 2016 election when Donald Trump lost the popular vote but won the electoral college (something that had happened to prior Republican presidents, such as George W. Bush in his race against Al Gore). In the aftermath of the election, Trump started to question the popular vote count and, as president, even established the Presidential Advisory Commission on Election Integrity, also known as the Pence-Kobach Voter Commission, to investigate so-called voter fraud in the 2016 election. (The Commission was disbanded in the face of legal challenges, including one that my Democracy Forward colleagues and I filed.) While the commission never found an instance of fraud, the seeds of voter denialism and conspiracy theories around voting had been planted. So during the 2020 election when Donald Trump, his lawyers, and his supporters argued that the election results that led to Joe Biden becoming president had been "rigged," there was support in place for the conspiracy. Those beliefs reached a boiling point on January 6, 2021, when violent rioters and insurrectionists sought to prevent the certification of the election by attacking the U.S. Capitol. This direct attack on the rule of law aimed to disrupt the peaceful transfer of power, an attack on democracy itself.

Congress has not stepped in to pass laws to comprehensively protect voting rights—even in the midst of January 6 or the weakening of the VRA. Now, President Trump has pardoned violent rioters and insurrectionists and continues to fan the flames of persistent and increasing election subversion. At the state level, laws that have been passed previously to expand the right to vote by making voting easier have faced anti-voting legal challenges. And, across the nation, many states continue to pass a range of maps and voting laws that restrict the right to vote. The latest threats include the president's transparent attempt to encourage off-cycle redistricting to win seats for his party; the concerning demands the Department of Justice has made for voter data; and the U.S. Supreme Court's decision in *Louisiana v. Callais,* which effectively eviscerates protections in Section 2 of the Voting Rights Act, a provision that played a critical role in ensuring fair voting opportunities for voters of color, especially in the South. As Justice Elena Kagan noted in her dissent, the Court's decision "threatens a half-century's worth of gains in voting equality." As we reflect on how we got here and the erosion of voting rights, it is important that we as ordinary people do our part to protect and expand the right to vote. Below are some ways to do so—from what you can do in under an hour to longer-term commitments.

TO-DO LIST

Ways to Support Voting Rights

(from the obvious-but-still-important to the more innovative)

Find a few actions that speak to you, and try them!

For more information on all below points, check out ordinarypeopleaction.com.

WHAT YOU CAN DO IN UNDER AN HOUR

→ **Make sure you are registered to vote and that you are tracking when elections are taking place.** You can find your polling place at vote.org or Vote411.org. You can check if you are registered to vote at vote.org.

➔ **Subscribe to a reliable listserv that will give you up-to-date, accurate information regarding voting rights.** I subscribe to *Democracy Docket* (democracydocket.com). This site also provides up-to-date information regarding threats to our elections and ways people can take action.

IF YOU HAVE MORE TIME

➔ **Pay attention to all elections, not just large national ones.** Even if there is not a nationally significant election, there could be an important state or local election. You can log on to Vote411.org to learn more about the elections in your area. Block some time off in your calendar to learn about candidates.

➔ **Talk with your friends and community members about voting. Make sure they are registered.** Offer to help register and keep them informed of when voting will occur. While this may seem minimal, you would be surprised how many people need encouragement to vote or make a plan.

➔ **Part of "making a plan" to vote is to know your rights and tell others about their rights.** Find specific information about how you can vote in your state at Vote411.org. Know your rights (e.g., you likely have the right to vote without showing your ID) and inform others of their rights. Make a plan for how to confront a situation in which your rights or the rights of other voters are violated.

→ **Be sure to go to ordinarypeopleaction.com to learn about ongoing efforts to threaten our elections and how to take specific actions to protect them.**

WHAT YOU CAN DO IN LESS THAN A DAY

→ **Be informed and support federal voting rights legislation and support laws,** such as the John R. Lewis Voting Rights Advancement Act of 2025, that protect and expand voting protections.

→ **Participate in voting marches, protests, and demonstrations** to oppose any effort to subvert elections or threaten the right to vote. Support the need for voting rights legislation and voter protections.

→ **Learn about your state laws too.** States can pass pro–voting rights legislation. Contact your state representatives to let them know you support these efforts.

→ **Writing to your member of Congress persistently about this priority is important.** You should also write to state representatives about your state's voting laws. Even if nothing happens overnight, it lets them know you are watching and care.

→ **Attend or create "town halls,"** and if your elected leader is not participating in town halls, host an "empty chair" town hall. (Resources on how to do this are listed on the ordinarypeopleaction.com website.)

→ **Write and submit articles and opinion pieces** to your local newspaper or make digital content (reels, videos) about the importance of voting, how to vote, and any reforms that are needed. Celebrate those who are working to protect the right to vote but, importantly, name and call out lawmakers who are not working *urgently* to protect the right to vote.

IF YOU HAVE A DAY OR A WEEKEND

- ➔ **Volunteer to register people to vote.** You can find opportunities to do this through Vote411.org or organizations you support that run voter awareness drives.
- ➔ **On Election Days and early voting days, accompany people to the polls** who may fear potential encounters with vote suppressors; make voting a fun, community event.
- ➔ **Volunteer to canvass voters.** Canvassing is going door-to-door to have conversations about important issues. Canvassing can increase voter turnout substantially. You can find information on how to canvass and canvassing opportunities at ordinarypeopleaction.com.

MORE ACTIONS

- ➔ **If you are a small business owner or in leadership at a company or organization, consider giving your employees time off for voting.**
- ➔ **Consider becoming a local election worker.** Your county website should have information on how to engage. HelpAmericaVote.gov has traditionally provided accurate and helpful information to encourage participation; you should check it out but be vigilant in monitoring the administration's actions to ensure the information stays reliable.

- ➔ **Plan a gathering for friends, colleagues, and community members** but ask that they show their "I voted" sticker (or a selfie of them wearing one) in order to attend the gathering.

- ➔ **Learn about efforts to "rewrite" history** (e.g., state laws that are teaching students that the 2020 election was rigged) and find ways to provide accurate education to people of all ages. (Some thoughts on how to engage in these efforts in your community are discussed in Action 3.)

- ➔ **If you are in high school, host a voter drive at your school.** Learn more about The Civics Center's Cap, Gown & Ballot initiative, which ensures that young people are registered to vote before they leave high school at thecivicscenter.org/cap-gown-and-ballot.

Spiral #2: Weakening of Checks and Balances. Over the past decade, our system of checks and balances has weakened. Researchers have cited a failure of Congress to provide checks on executive power as another reason the nation is facing a democratic backslide. In the past year, we have seen the Supreme Court at times shirk its responsibility to provide a check to the president's abuses of executive power (read more about this in Action 7). These failures, combined with rising extremism in a number of state legislatures, has weakened the checks and balances in our system, making it easier for an extreme political movement to consolidate power and rob the people of their freedom.

Spiral #3: Rising Inequality of Opportunity. In addition to the erosion of voting rights and the weakening of our checks and balances, the widening wealth gap has contributed to our democratic backslide. As noted above, equality (which includes equality of opportunity) is essential to a healthy democracy. In recent years, however, equality of opportunity has been declining. The wealthiest people of the nation's wealthy class are experiencing levels of increasing wealth not seen since the pre–Great Depression 1920s. Many people in the country work multiple jobs but still cannot make basic ends meet. At the same time the top 10 percent of households enjoy 70 percent of the nation's wealth, the bottom half of U.S. households hold less than 3 percent. In addition, the top 1 percent of U.S. households own about 30 percent of total wealth in the United States.[11] The number of people among the "working poor" has continued to rise as the wealth of the very few has increased. Today, the middle class is virtually nonexistent.

The lack of economic prosperity and the disappearance of the middle class creates major threats for our freedom and ability to thrive. Economic inequality combined with already disenfranchising voter laws creates situations in which large percentages of our population "opt out" of civic engagement. This means that only some voices are being heard in government and that our systems and institutions are not delivering for all people. Recent research from scholars at the University of Chicago traces the rise in economic inequality in nations like the United States to declines in robust democratic protections.[12]

It is imperative that our nation has opportunities for all people to thrive and that our government works to remove systemic barriers that keep hard working people from being able to prosper. But, until that happens, the well-justified lack of confidence in our government to deliver for working people provides a breeding ground of distrust, conspiracy, and misinformation as people look for someone to blame. The widening and unsustainable wealth gap has created fertile ground for anti-democracy and autocratic movements to grow.

TIP SHEET AND TO-DO LIST

Ways to Address the Wealth Gap

Dive deeper into what you can do to take action to help close the wealth gap. Start by getting the facts and then visit ordinarypeopleaction.com for how to take action.

- **Know the federal minimum wage.** The federal minimum wage is currently $7.25 per hour. This means that if you work forty hours a week for an entire year, you are making $15,080 before taxes. Or, $280 a week before taxes. This is not enough to live on in the United States without additional supports.
- **Know the minimum wage in your state.** The National Council of State Legislatures and other organizations provide charts that show the minimum wage in your state. Look one up (e.g., ncsl.org/labor-and-employment/state-minimum-wages) and know it. These wages are rarely living wages—meaning people work but cannot make ends meet. Having this information can equip you in the push for changes to wage laws and provide context when interacting with people day to day.
- **Take action to hold corporations accountable.** As the wealth gap widens, it is not just the government but also mega-corporations that need to be held accountable for the working conditions they create. Throughout history, ordinary people have been able to use their power to change working conditions, and we must do so now (more on the tools to do this in Action 6).

Spiral #4: Threats to Personal Freedom. Autocratic actors often seek to constrain personal freedom, and we have seen this trend in the Trump-Vance administration and in certain state and local governments. The administration has claimed that people cannot speak out in peaceful protest (a violation of the First Amendment), has sought to penalize institutions if their beliefs don't conform with the White House's agenda (a violation of the First Amendment), and is intent on undermining the freedom of the press (see Action 2). While the courts have provided strong guardrails against these incursions so far (although, as we discuss in Action 6, the Supreme Court has restricted personal liberty in some contexts, including in abortion), these threats are here and they are real. In Action 3, we dive into similar threats at the state and local levels with the rise in book bans and censorship. When personal liberty is threatened by the government, it can be a sign of declining democratic values.

Spiral #5: Threats to Due Process and the Rule of Law. Autocratic actors look for ways to undermine any checks on their power. We have seen this play out in the Trump-Vance administration when it has tried to skirt or not follow a number of court orders, denied people in immigration centers access to lawyers, and actively deprived people of due process. This is the mark of a democracy backsliding into autocracy.

TO-DO LIST

Explore the Ten Steps of Autocracy and Ten Steps to Freedom

Voting rights advocate and national leader Stacey Abrams and many other advocates have launched a national effort to ensure people understand the steps to autocracy and the steps that can be used to oppose autocracy and build freedom. Learning more and taking action through the 10 Steps Campaign is a great way to get started.

- ➔ Log on to 10stepscampaign.org.
- ➔ Consider how you can be part of the freedom steps.
- ➔ Sign up for action.
- ➔ Share with your friends.

Spiral #6: Global Threats to Our Freedom. The trends we see in the United States are not unique. Across the globe, there are more societies autocratizing than democratizing, and around the world many democracies have begun to backslide. A slow but concerning creep of authoritarianism is on the rise. Charismatic leaders use the discontent that people feel, whether due to the lack of economic opportunity or the failure of governmental and civic systems to deliver what they need, to falsely place blame on the "other." They frequently target or scapegoat groups of people (immigrants, people of color, marginalized communities) or cultural movements ("woke" academics), creating polarization that enables a rise of autocratic power.

TIP SHEET

How to answer claims (maybe by your loud relative at Thanksgiving) that "someone elected by the people cannot be anti-democratic; they are fulfilling the people's will":

- **A leader, in fact, can be elected by the people and then violate the people's rights.**
- **A leader also can be elected by people and be an anti-democratic, autocratic actor.**
- **Elections do not guarantee freedom or democracy.** Putin's Russia has elections but is not a free society. In addition, in places (like the United States) where votes are suppressed, elections are not as fair as they would be without voter suppression. This threatens freedom and democracy.

A rising political trend known as "competitive authoritarianism" is growing across the world. Charismatic leaders are elected when, on a large-scale, voters are feeling dissatisfaction with their lives and the way their country is delivering for them. Some of these leaders then exploit weaknesses in institutions or rights-protection frameworks (the Constitution, etc.) to consolidate and wield power in ways that restrict freedom.

How to answer claims that "criticizing your government is unpatriotic":

- **There is a difference between patriotism and nationalism.** Patriotism is born out of a love of our nation, its values, and its people—and recognizes that sometimes the highest form of loving one's country is being truthful about it and, yes, criticizing leaders and governments that don't live up to the nation's promises. This is known as patriotic dissent—and, as you will see discussed in this book, it is a key way to take action.

Nationalism is a concept that originated in the eighteenth-century and is about devotion to one's country and power often without regard to the character of the nation. Nationalism can often be divisive, encouraging discord between nations as well as division between a nation's communities. As we will see, anti-democratic movements are often nationalistic.

➔ **For resources on the difference between patriotism and nationalism visit ordinarypeopleaction.com.**

DEMOCRACY IS NOT A SPECTATOR SPORT

With an understanding of where we are, and the extent of the threat to our freedom, it's time to get intentional . . . and pick up a shovel. We must shift from being spectators to being players. Less talk, more action. Less spiraling, more problem solving. This is easier said than done because our current—increasingly online—world makes it easy to be a spectator.

What is a spectator? Spectators are onlookers who are not in the game—and we are all spectators from time to time. As spectators, we listen to or read the news or are flooded with a barrage of social media posts and then become overwhelmed by what is happening. We worry about what will happen if the president fails to follow an order of the Supreme Court or the Court fails to protect our rights. We become convinced that there is nothing we can do and throw up our hands. We may discuss with our friends and family or even write articles and make content about the intensity of ongoing events, about how terrible things are, but we skip over the part where we find solutions. As spectators, we may give into the whisper we all hear in the back of our minds asking "Does my voice matter? Can I really do anything? Why speak up when I can only see risk for doing so?"

Some spectators may retreat into their personal lives and disengage from civic life altogether. And many, especially those from more privileged backgrounds, choose to ignore what's going on because they believe it doesn't affect them. That they believe the infractions on people's rights only happen to others.

But the time for thinking that any of us is above our civic duty has passed: we must take action to defend our rights and the rights of others. There is no other time but now to do something about it.

Shifting Our Mindset from Spectators to Agents of Change. The late Congresswoman Barbara Jordan from Texas, who was the first Black woman from a Southern state elected to Congress and active in the fight for voting and civil rights and in holding President Nixon accountable in Watergate, would always say that the stakes were too high for government to be a spectator sport.[13] That is true not just with government but with our society overall. *The stakes are now too high for our democracy to be a spectator sport.*

We must resist the temptation to watch the decline of our democracy from our phones and sit by while our communities deteriorate. Meeting this moment requires that we become someone who acts in the face of what is happening. This mindset shift can be difficult, but it is essential for us to alter the trajectory of our democracy. There are many things that we cannot control, that may seem too big and sweeping, but the truth is we *can* control how we respond. In focusing on our power to respond, we transform ourselves from spectators to agents of change.

In 1910, President Theodore Roosevelt addressed an audience at the most prestigious university in Paris, where he discussed the role of citizens in a democratic republic. He warned that cynics—who believe there is nothing that can be done to change their circumstances and so refrain from acting—do not advance democracy. He further cautioned that cynicism is often most prevalent within elite circles, such as theirs, in which people make a range of arguments and offer a host of reasons for why they cannot make change. He then highlighted that, unlike in nations where power is vested with one or a few people, democratic republics vest power with the people. That means, he said, "in the long run, success or failure" of democracy "will be conditioned upon the way in which the average man, the average woman, does his or her duty, first in the ordinary, every-day affairs of life, and next in those great occasional cries which call for the heroic virtues."[14] Decades later, Congresswoman Jordan echoed this call: "For the American idea, though it is shared by all of us, is realized in each one of us."[15]

Freedom isn't something that is handed down by a government, it is something that all people possess. We all have the ability to be agents, not onlookers, and we must actively work to shift our mindset away from being in the bleachers. We must get into the action.

Sociologist and author Tressie McMillan Cottom recently said, "We are getting so much passive information, and we have so few opportunities to act. We are tired then, not from doing too much, but from doing too little."[16] She also said, "The more time you spend doing something . . . the less exhausted you are by the onslaught of information that really wins when it can convince you that the only thing you can do is watch what is happening to you."[17]

The chapters that follow explore all of the ways that we can act after we make this critical mindset shift. Democracy is not a spectator sport.

SHIFTING THE MINDSET

The chart below provides examples of how we must make this mindset shift. More information can be found at ordinarypeopleaction.com.

Spectator Mindset	Agent Mindset
• Doomscrolling • Catastrophizing • Thinking what is happening in the news won't happen to you • Disengaging in your community • Refusing to vote or be civically active because you don't feel represented • Focusing only on national events and being overwhelmed, with no energy to focus on local community needs • Feeling isolated	• Finding ways to be informed (see Action 2, page 63) and then translating concern into small, repeatable actionable steps • Making a plan for how you will know and defend your rights when you begin catastrophizing (see Action 3, page 85) • Examining needs in your community and taking action (see Action 3, page 85) • Building community and connecting to prevent feeling alone and disengaged • Considering ways to encourage people you believe in to engage in civic life or run for office (Actions 2, page 63, and 3, page 85)

Now, think about a few ways in which you may be a spectator and how you can shift your mindset in response. Then, fill out this chart.

My spectator mindset (worries, fears, observations)	How I can reframe my mindset to being an agent of change

TIP SHEET

How to Talk with Children About What Is Happening in the United States

For more information go to: ordinarypeopleaction.com/kidscorner.

- **Begin early and talk often.** This is not one conversation but a continued conversation about power, justice, identity, and resilience.
- **Focus the conversation on instilling resilience, values, and a vision.** Help the child find pride in who they are and in their heritage with stories of resilience and identity. (These stories will differ depending on the child's background and the lived experiences of the child's parents, ancestors, and community members.)
- **Ground the conversation in your shared values.** For example, "We care about the ability of all people to have freedom and thrive." "We believe that the future should be better than the present and the past and care about your ability to have a good future." "In our family, we believe in kindness." "In our family, our ancestors overcame."
- **Use age-appropriate, factual information about what is happening.** Do not sugarcoat, but focus the conversation on how you and your family/community are responding to what is happening. ("I want to talk with you about why we/our friends are afraid to be outside." "I want to talk with you about what you might experience at school." "I want to talk with you about why we, as a family, are spending Saturday to help people

register to vote." "I want you to know why we take time to go to your school board meeting." "I want you to know why we support our public library." "I want you to know why we are marching today.") This type of statement enables you to discuss the problems of society and what is happening while also focusing on what people are empowered to do about it.

→ **Partner with children in actions they can take and use those actions as part of the conversation.** This can include volunteer work, learning about a new topic relevant to what they are experiencing, advocating for changes in local or state spaces (schools), and building clubs or communities with friends, among other things.

→ **Set time for specific conversations that are necessary for the safety of the child and his or her community.** Conversations about what to do if ICE agents approach your school, church, or home—and how to interact with the police—are specific conversations that should be linked to these broader topics and often should be more direct and instructive.

Remember, you are not alone. Partner with community members and others in your orbit to have these conversations.

We are in an extraordinarily difficult time and the threats to our families, communities, our neighbors, and ourselves keep mounting. Yet what we do in response during this time will be what makes the difference. Democracy is a choice. Democracy requires that we are willing to be actors in society—that we insist on governing ourselves. Taking action does not just mean that we need people who vote or run for office every few years; it means that each of us must take responsibility to build the nation we wish to live in, to oppose attempts to restrict our freedom, and to support efforts to make freedom more accessible to our neighbors. The critical fights in our nation's history—from the Revolutionary War to the abolition of slavery to the fight against global fascism in World War II to the civil rights and workers' rights movements and so many more—were not won by the powerful. They were won by ordinary people. People who demanded more, and better. Democracy depends on ordinary people realizing their power and making decisions about what to do in the face of their day-to-day circumstances. It requires that we pick up a shovel. Democracy is not a spectator sport.

ACTION 2

Achieve Information Sobriety

"IT WON'T BE NEWSWORTHY UNTIL SOMEONE DIES WHILE ATTENDING WORSHIP OR A RELIGIOUS SERVICE." This was the feedback our team at Democracy Forward received from a major news outlet when we talked with them about covering a case about to be filed by our clients—a coalition of Baptist churches, Quaker meeting houses, and a Sikh gurdwara. It was in the early weeks of President Trump's second term, and we were challenging the administration's decision to overturn a policy that had been in place for more than thirty years to protect sensitive locations (such as hospitals, schools, and churches) from indiscriminate immigration raids by ICE agents. The policy had stood during both Democratic and Republican administrations (including Trump's first administration) and had protected the religious rights and liberties of people in vulnerable civil society locations. Rescinding the policy so that immigrant communities were scared to access healthcare or education or attend worship services, was especially cruel. Our team was particularly focused on houses of worship in those early days because of concerns we had heard from religious leaders across the nation that their communities would no longer be able to worship together, heightening their fear of isolation during an uncertain time.

Five days after the administration reversed the protection for these sensitive locations, ICE agents raided a church in Atlanta, Georgia, disrupting a religious service and taking one of the congregants into custody—a man who had been in the country for more than two decades, working six days a week, and keeping every immigration court date required of him. The pastor of the church described the disruptive nature of the operation and how deeply it had impacted his congregation's ability to worship. The abrupt and unreasoned policy change, and the actions it unleashed, had houses of worship and worshipers, including our clients, feeling scared and on edge. The administration's actions were unlawful, and we were working quickly to file a lawsuit.

It is customary for our team to tell our clients' stories through the media so the public can know what is happening to their fellow Americans. We wanted to tell people the story of our lawsuit challenging the administration for enabling such actions in contravention of thirty years of U.S. policy. We were shocked to receive the response from media outlets that this story was not sexy enough for news coverage unless accompanied by death or injury. Sadly, people not being able to worship freely was deemed not newsworthy.

We filed the case anyway, as our clients needed to be protected from the threats of raids. We found an outlet that would cover the case when it was filed. We won the first federal court order in the nation finding that the president's policy was likely unlawful—an arbitrary violation of religious liberty—and we have only picked up steam since then.

THE NEED FOR INFORMATION SOBRIETY

The chilling suggestion that our lawsuit was not newsworthy unless someone participating in the lawsuit had already died or been hurt in a church raid has stayed with me. It confirms what many of us believe about the current media landscape: It runs on sensationalism and outrage (two things that generate advertising revenues), and—more often than not—the number of clicks a story or post will likely get determines whether it will be published. This leaves important stories untold and voices unheard, and it creates a frenzy of news consumption for sensationalized topics.

If you are feeling overwhelmed by and unsure about the constant deluge of media coverage, you are not alone. According to the Pew Research Center, Americans of all ideological backgrounds are increasingly distrustful of national media outlets. Americans differ, depending on their political backgrounds and persuasions, on which national news sources they find most trustworthy.[1] In general, the Weather Channel is considered trustworthy[2] and there is alignment on the reliability of financial news sources, but for news regarding political and social issues there are deep divisions between Americans on which sources to believe.[3] Even trust in local media organizations, while higher than that in national media outlets, has also dropped in recent years. As of 2021, an increasing number of people (approximately 40 percent of Americans and large portions of younger Americans) are turning to social media for their news and information, even as they find social media to be the least trustworthy of all news sources.[4]

Making the mind shift from spectator to agent of change requires addressing our collective and individual media consumption with an aim to achieve information sobriety. By this, I mean acknowledging how information affects us and being intentional about how we consume news and what we do with it. If we are not well-informed, we are hindered in our ability to fully assess what is happening to our communities and our country and, ultimately, in our ability to take action. Being well informed and knowing the facts is an action we must take in this time; indeed, it is foundational to taking the other actions in this book. We must achieve information sobriety.

Each person needs to make a plan for how to take in information: How do we stay informed without becoming so overwhelmed that we become paralyzed and are unable to take action? How do we check the information we are being fed (and understand that we *are* being fed)? The plan should include how to support independent media and investigative journalism that runs on substance not sensation. In addition, we should increase our awareness of news sources and sub-sources and be wary of narratives and "developments" that obscure important details and context. Being alert to manipulation is an important skill to develop. Each of us needs to become an active, purposeful seeker of information rather than passively absorb whatever comes our way.

One of the first aspects to consider is how to distinguish between information, misinformation, and disinformation. While we live in a time when it is easier than ever to explore new ideas and dive deep into many issues, we also live in a time when the amount of information can be overwhelming and challenging. Managing reality means wading through an ever-growing mountain of disinformation and misinformation.

To achieve information sobriety, we must first explore how our media environment interfaces with our everyday lives and how those who seek to influence our democracy use the media for good and bad.

What is misinformation? Misinformation is inaccurate information or false information—but it is not shared or spread with malicious intent (though it can still be harmful).

What is disinformation? Disinformation is false information that is put into the world with the *intention* of misleading people.

Both misinformation and disinformation are concerning—and both are intensified by the expansion of digital media distribution platforms, the increasing prevalence of AI-generated content, and bots designed specifically to disseminate mis- and disinformation.

Importance of a Free Press and How Anti-Democratic Actors Undermine the Free Press. The ability to report facts, publish information, and express opinions, even criticism, without government restraint is a cornerstone of a democracy. Freedom of the press is critical to holding governments accountable, keeping those in power in check, maintaining an informed public, and preventing the spread of misinformation.

In the United States, these roles date back to before the end of the Revolutionary War when Samuel Adams criticized British control of Boston in the *Boston Gazette* news columns in the late 1700s.[5] At the time, these publications were considered radical and inflammatory. Some years later, in 1791, when the Bill of Rights was added to the United States Constitution, the First Amendment would recognize freedom of the press as a central right of the people. For centuries since our founding, the free press (meaning a press corps free of financial or political influence from those in power) has exposed the negative conditions in which people live, corruption in government (such as the press's role in publishing the Pentagon Papers, exposing Watergate scandals, and reporting NSA surveillance), and who has undue influence with the government.

Exerting control over the media environment and quashing media that criticizes those in power is a hallmark of political leaders who seek to consolidate power away from the people. We have seen this throughout history. Prior to the invention of the Gutenberg printing press circa 1450, the Catholic Church controlled most of the information disseminated throughout Europe. As a result, church authorities often manipulated the content before it reached the people. For centuries after, monarchies and seats of political power manipulated information in Europe through state-controlled media that censored criticism of the government. This continues to be a feature of anti-democratic regimes, including China, North Korea, Putin's Russia, and the Taliban's Afghanistan.

In 2010, as Viktor Orbán came to power in Hungary, his allies began buying news outlets in the country. By 2016, one of the country's most prominent newspapers, *Népszabadság* (which means "The People's Liberty"), was shut down after being purchased by a financier with links to Orbán. Reporters Without Borders has expressed concern that Orbán and his allies built "a true media empire subject to his party's orders" that controls more than 80 percent of Hungary's media market and pushes pro-government propaganda.[6] These efforts have moved beyond television and newspapers to social media platforms, where the government continues to advertise and drive the flow of information and disinformation.

Current Threats to Press Freedom in the United States. The United States is not immune from threats to the free press. For public debate to be as robust as possible, it is important that a wide range of media sources, editors, writers, podcasters, producers, and media outlets can fully engage with ideas and perspectives. One irony of the modern moment is that even though information is more accessible than it has ever been—with the advent of 24-hour news and the proliferation of the internet and social and digital media—the number of those who control the sources of this information has become fewer, threatening the independence of the press.

Over the last few decades, media ownership has been consolidated, resulting in several major corporate institutions now controlling the vast majority of media outlets in the United States. In 1983, fifty companies owned 90 percent of the U.S. media. Now there are just six major media companies—Comcast, The Walt Disney Company, Warner Bros. Discovery, Paramount Skydance, Sony, and Amazon. As of this writing, Paramount Skydance is seeking to take over Warner Bros. Discovery, which would result in further consolidation.[7] The Federal Communications Commission (FCC), under the leadership of Trump-appointed chair Brendan Carr, is also attempting to let NexStar, a company that owns hundreds of television stations in the U.S., expand. (Our team at Democracy Forward is challenging the expansion, as this book is going to print.) In *The New Media Monopoly,* author Ben Bagdikian (who warned of rising media consolidation back in 1983) observes that the consolidation of media power in the United States gives leaders of corporations more communications power than has ever been exercised by "any despot or dictatorship in history."[8]

This means that while it seems we may have access to more news and information than previously, much of it is influenced by large media conglomerates that are aligned with those in power. Maximizing profits and pacifying those in power results in actions that undermine truth-telling and important criticism of the government. This centralized system can also mean that targeting or pressuring just one media institution by those in power has significant implications for the larger media landscape, as ripple effects impact affiliates and smaller companies within the organization. We have witnessed this phenomenon during the Trump-Vance administration's first year in office.

The president and his allies' early attack on ABC (now under parent company The Walt Disney Company) regarding Jimmy Kimmel is a prime example of this phenomenon. Kimmel's monologue after the killing of conservative activist Charlie Kirk angered President Trump and his allies. Many of the president's supporters called on ABC to suspend Kimmel's show. To compound the pressure, Brendan Carr and the FCC, which is supposed to be an *independent* agency, threatened possible retributory action against ABC if Kimmel was not suspended. This raised major First Amendment red flags (the government cannot penalize the media for the content of its speech under our Constitution) and concerns about the independence of the FCC. It demonstrated for us how governmental pressure on a media institution can shape what information the public receives.

ABC initially capitulated to the president's demands and suspended Kimmel, a move celebrated by the president. Yet massive public outcry from ordinary people taking action to boycott ABC and Disney forced the media company to change its mind—and *Jimmy Kimmel Live!* was broadcast again. The incident illustrates how quickly a political actor intent on quashing dissent can manipulate the consolidated media environment—but it also showed how ordinary people can fight back. Other noteworthy incidents have occurred with CBS (Paramount Skydance), Comcast, and the BBC.

Media manipulation didn't start with President Trump but has accelerated since his inauguration, with many who enable him exploiting their control over the media to align with his preferences. Prior to the 2024 election, the editorial boards of *The Washington Post* and the *Los Angeles Times,* both now owned by billionaires, declined to endorse presidential candidates, a break in a decades-long tradition of providing the public with thoughtful analysis about the strengths of their preferred candidate. The decisions were made by their owners, who put their own business interests first, concerned that an endorsement of Vice President Harris might anger Trump if he were elected. The move to silence the editorial boards was especially ironic for *The Post,* whose motto is "Democracy Dies in Darkness." These developments suggest that we may be closer to an Orbán-like takeover of the media in the United States than many of us realize—as well as underlining the importance of ordinary people using their voices to push back against this growing threat.

After his inauguration, President Trump signed a bill pushed by Republicans in Congress that cut $9 billion in public broadcast funding, including more than $1 billion for the Corporation for Public Broadcasting, which had to close its doors in early 2026. These funds have historically supported many media outlets on which the public relies, including Public Broadcasting Service (PBS) and National Public Radio (NPR), and more than 1,500 locally owned stations. The president has accused stations such as PBS and NPR of failing to create "fair, accurate, and unbiased" reporting, and Voice of America for promoting a radical anti-Trump agenda. He has also blocked the Associated Press from attending some White House events and has continually used White House social media platforms to criticize and demean journalists and the media. Federal agents arrested journalists (including Don Lemon) in Minnesota. The attacks have been especially prevalent for women and Black journalists. Creators, who often serve as "citizen journalists," have also been targeted and attacked simply for recording what the government is doing in our communities. The president has gone so far as to support calls that people should be hanged for their speech if it portrays him in a negative light.[9] While many of these actions are unlawful and should (and likely will) be stopped by the courts, they are nevertheless creating chilling effects across the nation's press and destabilizing a fragile media environment.

Threats from the Prevalence of Big Tech and Social Media Platforms. Social media enables many of us to obtain quicker real-time information that can, if accurate, be tremendously helpful. Yet social media can simultaneously overwhelm us with an onslaught of data and carries a high risk for misinformation and disinformation. Big Tech algorithms (aided by AI that is programmed to feed us news and events that are tied to profit) control the flow of information to our phones and devices in ways that are challenging to disrupt. Large tech companies such as Google, Meta, Apple, and Amazon play huge roles in our media consumption and shape so much of what we see and experience online. Today the internet reaches more people in the United States than ever before, but much of the content that reaches us is increasingly coming from a few consolidated entities. The negative content control results of a consolidated broadcast media ecosystem are being replicated by the consolidation of tech platforms that control what we can view. Many companies have chosen to align with the administration, which has channeled government funding their way in the hopes of receiving loyalty. Companies have been rewarded with executive orders that increase their profits. To interpret the content being fed to us, we have to be intentional about what we are consuming.

How This Affects Us: News, Social Media, and Mental Health. Researchers have found that consuming large amounts of news and social media is associated with depression and anxiety, especially in teens and young adults.[10] This can translate into a sense of fear and paralysis that can inhibit the ability of ordinary people to make change in their communities and can weaken our democracy as a whole.

SIX STEPS TO ACHIEVE INFORMATION SOBRIETY

To maintain a healthy balance of staying informed without experiencing a sense of being overwhelmed by too much information, these steps will help you understand the impact that media has on your mental health, how to take stock of your current habits, and how to change as necessary. Achieving information sobriety is an action we can—and should—take, especially in this extraordinary time.

1. Take an Information Inventory. The first step is becoming aware of your current practice through reflection and taking inventory of how you consume media. Write down where you get your news and what information you obtain. Record the amount of time you spend interacting with all sources including social media, radio, television, print news, podcasts, and newsletters. Be sure to include in your inventory "invisible influences," such as news or information you may take in without intending to (e.g., a television that is on constantly in your office, mindless social media scrolling, group text chains). The questions that follow will help you with your inventory.

Information Inventory

Consider your answers to these questions over the course of a day or week.

As you encounter information or media, jot down your habits. It may be helpful to discuss with a friend or loved one.

- ➔ Do you make an effort to stay informed about current events? If so, how? If not, why?

- What type of and how much information do you need to feel informed on a daily basis? A weekly basis?
- Where/how do you get your news? Through which devices and mediums? During what hours do you consume news?
- What information do you want but you are not getting? What information are you getting that you don't want?
- How do you feel when you consume news?
- How long do you spend scrolling through social media? How many news stories or how much information about current events do you see in your feeds (intentionally or unintentionally)? Are there other unintentional sources of information you're receiving? (Water cooler, subway ads, that TV in the office.)
- Do you have any relationships that center discussion of current events as the main means of communication? (Sometimes this can take the form of group chats with friends.)
- Do you read any newsletters or e-news? Other commentaries (see page 78 for definition)? From where?
- Do you listen to or interface with any commentary or sources of news that challenge your worldview?
- Do you follow any local news (see page 77 for definition)? Local television stations? Local paper? Blogs or posts from local writers?
- Are any of the sources of media you read or listen to from independent news media sources (see page 76 for definition)?

- → What times of day and days of the week do you feel most energized and able to take in information? What times are not good for you to get information?
- → Are there sources of news that you would recommend to a friend? Which ones and why?

2. Assess Your Information Inventory and Give Yourself Permission to Change Your Media Habits. As you assess your inventory, pay specific attention to questions regarding how you *feel* when you are interacting with information, and also take note of the different ways in which you interface with information. Many people do not realize just how much information they are unintentionally absorbing through social media or other mediums and how that affects their mood and outlook. Others may consider themselves "news junkies" but are not consuming information from a wider range of varying sources, which would give them a more holistic picture with fuller context. As you reflect on your inventory, give yourself permission to rethink and change your habits and viewpoints.

Permission Slip

The goal is to find a healthy balance that allows you to stay informed in a way that motivates you to take action. If the media you consume leaves you feeling overwhelmed or hopeless, it may be time to pull back or find alternative sources.

PERMISSION SLIP

- ➔ It's okay for me to change my media consumption.
- ➔ It's okay for me to log off social media if I find it overwhelming.
- ➔ It's okay for me to find alternate news sources that I trust.
- ➔ It's okay to communicate my needs to others surrounding the news, whether that be to ask for more earnest conversations about current events or to request that we find other topics to discuss.
- ➔ It's okay for me to get overwhelmed by the sensationalist, 24-hour news cycle, and find a source that works better for me.

3. Make a Plan for a Well-Balanced Media Diet. With the information from your personal inventory in mind, make a plan to rebalance (or, if you feel you have it just right, reaffirm) your media diet to ensure varied sources and accurate information without overload. A few concepts regarding media sources are important to review.

Media Sources You Should Know

More information on media sources can be found at ordinarypeopleaction.com.

Independent media. Independent media refers to media outlets (websites, TV stations or programs, newspapers, magazines, podcasts, other newsletters) that operate without influence from large corporations or the government. They are generally seen as more willing to invest in quality investigative journalism, tend to avoid sensationalism, and do not feel pressured to make coverage choices based on the interest of power structures. By selecting independent media sources, you can make certain that you receive factual information that is as free as possible from corporate or governmental pressure. News aggregator sites such as trustworthymedia.org provide an excellent starting place in accessing independent media sources.

Local journalism. Local journalism is broadly defined as reporting news for a specific geographic area or community. Local journalism is not necessarily independent journalism, but it can be. It can come in the form of newspapers, television, radio, blogs, newsletters, magazines, and social media accounts. In recent years local journalism has been on the decline as communities have faced underinvestment and larger media conglomerates have purchased local news channels, making them less trustworthy sources for local factual news. As a result, finding sources of local news can be difficult depending on where you live and your community. A recent study by Muck Rack documented the radical decline in local media: Less than twenty-five years ago the United States had an average of about forty journalists per 100,000 residents and that number has now dropped by 75 percent to about eight. To mitigate against these changes, it can be helpful to get to know your local journalists or reporters through reaching out to them, perhaps arranging to have them speak to a local group in your community. Focusing on local news is good way of supporting your community.

Public broadcast. These are news sources like PBS and NPR that aim to make their content available for free to the public without influence of government or corporations. This is a form of independent media and, depending on the broadcast, can be a form of local journalism too. NPR and PBS take a combination of private donations, revenues from subscription services, and corporate and government grants—although they are designed with a firewall to prevent any external influence over their media coverage.

National media. National media refers to media sources that cover stories relevant to the entire nation. They include network and cable news like Fox News, CBS, or MS NOW; newspapers such as *The New York Times* and *USA Today;* news services like the Associated Press and National Public Radio (which is both national media and public broadcast); and a range of new digital media (like MeidasTouch Network) that are focused on national topics. National media can be independent or it can be corporate or governmentally controlled.

Investigative journalism. Investigative journalism involves journalists and reporters conducting a "deep dive" look into a specific topic, event, or occurrence. The goal is to go beyond explaining what happened to examine *why* it happened. Often this type of journalism seeks to hold powerful people or entities accountable and in this way it plays an important role in protecting the general public from abuses by the powerful. Historically, despite the limitations of the consolidated U.S. media ownership, investigative journalists have often relied on the robust media market in the United States and funding through federal programs to be able to conduct their work. The Trump-Vance administration has cut funds to these programs, threatening investigative journalism across the globe.

New media. New media refers to media that is digitally distributed—whether through podcasts, social media, YouTube, or websites. A creator or social media influencer who has a show or video that you like is an example of new media, as are organizations that send you media and information via emails or through social media or other digital channels. New media can be independent or it can be influenced by corporations and the government.

Commentary and opinion. While many media outlets are viewed as having an ideological bent (Fox News as an outlet that appeals to people who have traditionally supported Republicans and MS NOW as an outlet that appeals to people who have traditionally supported Democrats), it is important to remember that some information that is put out in the world, though often called "news," is simply commentary and opinion—where people offer their own views rather than aiming to report the facts. Reading commentary and opinion can be valuable, but it is important to understand that commentary and opinion are not a substitute for factual reporting.

Achieving information sobriety requires working to have a balanced media diet in which you consume varied sources of media. Achieving information sobriety will likely take some work, definitely requires vigilance regarding how you take in your news, and being especially intentional in seeking out new sources.

First, check that you are reading some sources of independent and local media, as they are going to be key drivers in a positive media diet.

Independent media sources will provide you with factual information that is as free as possible from corporate or governmental pressure. News aggregator sites such as trustworthymedia.org provide excellent starting points to independent media sources. Good outlets to consider are the Associated Press (AP), *ProPublica, Chalkbeat,* and *The Guardian*—as well as NPR and PBS. In addition, there are a range of independent sources of news and commentary that you may wish to explore depending on your interests and values. Consult ordinarypeopleaction.com for additional information.

Local journalism is also important. The late political comedian Mark Russell, who for years had a show on PBS, shared with me one of his tricks of the trade to connect with communities and people of all political backgrounds across the country. Whenever he visited a town or city to perform a show, he picked up a local newspaper and/or listened to the local news. This not only allowed him to understand what was happening in the local community, but also to get a broader perspective on what people there were experiencing and what mattered to them. Mark was on to something. There is a direct relationship between the strength of local journalism in an area and civic engagement and higher voter turnout—it is no coincidence that as local journalism has declined, so too have core aspects of our civic life.

Mixing in other sources of media can be important too. Just because a media outlet is owned by a large corporate entity does not mean that it is unreliable, but it does mean that we need to be cautious about what outside influences are deciding what news you are being fed or how developments are covered. In addition, bringing in sources of media that are of interest to you, whether digitally or through more traditional mediums, can help you identify what is missing. Be sure to aim for variety in the platforms you use to receive your news.

4. Plan Where and When to Get Your Information. The multiplicity of sources and the constant barrage of information can be overwhelming, putting us in a state of anxiety and depression, and ultimately lead us to inaction. In an effort to keep us up to date, many of us receive news alerts on our devices all day long, often putting us necessarily on edge. But do we really need to be tuned in so much? Probably not. Instead, use your inventory to determine what your information needs are and then make a plan to be proactive about when—and where—to get information. The idea is to put yourself in charge.

- **Identify your daily and weekly needs.** Pinpoint where on the informed spectrum you need to be, then schedule check-ins accordingly.

- **Identify news or social media blackout times.** Determine the times during the day (phone-free mornings or bedtimes) or week (such as weekends) when you can fully unplug.
- **Mind the chats.** Put limits on when you check or respond to group chats that share current events.
- **Get issue specific.** Make a plan to obtain information regarding specific issues of concern for you or that motivate you to act, while not feeling as if you need to keep up on every national and international issue. A list of subject matter newsletters and media options by topic is available on ordinarypeopleaction.com.

Your plan or approach may change over time based on the news and/or your different needs. The point is to set some limits and create some habits for yourself to avoid burning yourself out.

5. Be Curious and Explore. As a next step, be inquisitive and explore new media sources. Be open to recommendations from other people, especially if they expose you to perspectives of people who disagree with you. The goal is not to change your mind, just to provide points of comparison that help you be a more informed consumer of information.

TO-DO LIST

BE YOUR OWN FACT-CHECKER

→ **Sometimes you will need to investigate on your own whether the information you're getting is accurate.** This is especially true now, when some federal government websites, which used to contain accurate and helpful information, may no longer be reliably trusted.

- ➔ **Go to ordinarypeopleaction.com to explore methods of checking facts**—and how to identify reliable information and whether government websites contain misinformation or disinformation. With the tools lists, this task is not as difficult as it may seem, and it can give you confidence in the information and facts you are obtaining.

6. Take Actions to Support a Pro-Democracy Media Ecosystem. Achieving information sobriety requires each of us to recognize the power we have to contribute to and support a healthier media ecosystem. Below are some ways to get started.

HOW TO SUPPORT A HEALTHIER MEDIA ECOSYSTEM

IF YOU HAVE FIFTEEN MINUTES

- ➔ **Visit ordinarypeopleaction.com to familiarize yourself with independent sources of media.**
- ➔ **Consider donating to a nonprofit newsroom or buying a subscription to a source for independent news.**
- ➔ **Subscribe to your local newspaper** if it provides useful information and is a source of reliable news. Become a member of your local public broadcast service (PBS) station.

IF YOU HAVE AN HOUR

- **Familiarize yourself with organizations** like the American Journalism Project (theajp.org), Reporters Committee for Freedom of the Press (rcfp.org), the Society of Professional Journalists (spj.org), Civic News Company (civicnews.org), and others that support press freedom and independent or local journalism. Sign up for their updates.
- **Write a reporter or commentator who you believe has contributed positively to your understanding and perspective and thank them.** You can do this privately or through a public letter to the editor.
- **If there are creators or influencers that are credible (you can find a list of accounts to follow at ordinarypeopleaction.com), explore ways to support their work.**

IF YOU HAVE SOME MORE TIME

- **Get to know reporters in your local area.** Build a relationship with a local journalist or writer or get to know your local newsroom.
- **Host a gathering with friends where you all share a favorite writer or journalist or create a current events club** (like a book club) where you focus on a piece of investigative journalism.

OTHER ACTIONS TO CONSIDER (AND THINGS TO AVOID)

- **While AI and chatbots can be helpful, you should avoid using them as a source of news.** Support researchers and writers generating the information as a way of supporting a healthy media ecosystem. In addition, AI at times mis-summarizes the news or hallucinates (fabricating details) fake reporting. AI-based newsfeeds are built on algorithms, discussed above, that will often "reward" clicks and may only send you information that it perceives you may want to hear, hiding contrary information even if accurate and important in understanding reality.

→ **Learn about News Literacy Project and their work to equip educators to teach news literacy and independent thinkers.** Block off time to explore their resources and take action (you can access their program here: newslit.org). Find other aligned programs at ordinarypeopleaction.com.

Achieving an intentional approach to information and media consumption—achieving information sobriety—is important as we engage in this moment. It is important to be informed so that we understand what is going on without falling prey to misinformation, sensationalism, echo chambers, and constant conflict. With a plan in place for information sobriety, we can navigate a toxic media landscape with dexterity, allowing ourselves intentional interaction, the ability to obtain accurate and reliable information, and plenty of breathing room.

ACTION 3

Begin at Your Front Door

"THERE IS MORE THAN ONE WAY TO BURN A BOOK. AND THE WORLD IS FULL OF PEOPLE RUNNING ABOUT WITH LIT MATCHES."[1] This quote appears in *Fahrenheit 451*, Ray Bradbury's 1953 dystopian novel about a futuristic American society where books have been outlawed. In July 2023, a federal court order issued in Arkansas began with those same words.[2] The order blocked the enforcement of a law recently passed by the Arkansas legislature and signed by Governor Sarah Huckabee Sanders that would have placed criminal penalties on librarians for making books accessible to young people that could be deemed "harmful" to minors. While Arkansas didn't want to literally burn the books, a federal judge saw the state law for what it was: Another way to suppress written ideas—a pernicious part of authoritarianism that has crept back into American politics, one that threatens to take away one of our cherished freedoms in the First Amendment: to be able to obtain information without the government censoring it. Working alongside local lawyers and partners, our team at Democracy Forward had filed suit to block the law a month earlier.

It was through that work that I had the opportunity to meet Adam Webb. Adam would describe himself as an ordinary guy. He has lived in Arkansas his whole life, is a husband and a dad, has two dogs, and likes to fish. When he became a librarian, he didn't think his line of work would land him in court or at the center of one of the most essential fights for our democracy. Yet Adam's work as a public library administrator and his commitment to the rights of all people—including young people and teens—to read and be exposed to uncensored books and ideas put him squarely in a local fight with far-reaching implications.

Censorship and the Decline of Free Societies

The relationship between censorship and the decline of free societies has been well documented. In 1930s Germany, Nazi supporters publicly burned books proscribed as "un-German" and/or written by Jewish authors. The Nazis often used claims of "protecting innocent children" to justify the suppression of books and ideas that they considered inconsistent with their nationalist ideology. In contemporary times, Viktor Orbán's Hungary censored books, including those with LGBTQ themes. Other authoritarian countries, such as China, Russia, and Iran have restricted books and publishing for a long time. In the United States, book bans have been on the rise in recent years.

When people in power trample on individual rights, those rights can be protected only when someone has the courage to step forward to defend them. Adam is one of those people. As president of the Arkansas Library Association, he and a number of librarians, counties, and booksellers secured a court order that, as this book is going to print, has protected librarians throughout their state for two years.

You may feel that an issue happening far across the country doesn't affect where you live. But these local fights are emblematic of the dangers we all face across the country as our rights are eroded—and they are part of the solution to our larger crisis. Over the course of my work, I have met so many people like Adam Webb, whose courage has made a real difference in their communities. From parents who have stepped up to defend the rights of kids and teachers in their schools, to the Little League coach who stood between ICE agents and his team during baseball practice, to people who find ways to make their neighborhoods safer and kinder so that everyone feels as if they belong.

People like Adam know that the fight for our future lies right outside our own front door, and that this is where our power resides. This is true no matter where your real or metaphorical front door is. For Adam, he is determined to fight for the people in his local community—the kids who come to the library to lose themselves in stories, teens who are looking for a sense of belonging in characters just like them, for the librarians who love finding just the right book for someone—and for everyone's right to read. Elsewhere, we have seen local communities band together quite literally at their own front doors to protect one another from violent raids by the Trump administration's federal agents—the Minnesota neighborhoods that, as this book was being written, guarded their own streets and protected daycare centers and schools; the New Orleans neighbors who delivered meals and groceries to those who may be targeted or profiled by masked agents; the communities who built stronger bonds during wildfires and national disasters, creating a network of care.

The fight for democracy begins at our front doors, and we must each step outside if we are to save ourselves and our country.

COMMUNITIES ARE CRADLES OF DEMOCRACY

Too often, we think of democracy, political systems, and the change we want to see in our society as grandiose concepts consigned to far-off places with marbled halls in a state capitol or in Washington, D.C. In reality, our day-to-day interactions in our local communities weave the fabric of our democracy.

When French aristocrat and political thinker Alexis de Tocqueville came to the United States in the early 1800s to study democracy in our new nation, he observed that "the strength of free peoples" in the United States "resides in the local community." He wrote that "local institutions are to liberty what primary schools are to science; they put it within the people's reach . . . without local institutions a nation may give itself a free government, but it has not got the spirit of liberty."[3]

Tocqueville's observations have rung true through the various social movements that have improved our country over the centuries. Movements such as the abolitionist movement, the workers' rights movement, the civil rights movement, the suffrage movement, and many others all started with individuals who wanted to change their circumstances and took steps in their local communities to do so. Over time, these local actions grew into local movements and then larger national ones.

However, most of us do not think about our local communities in connection with the words "government" or "politics." According to recent surveys, most Americans associate these words only with the federal government. Yet local governments affect our daily lives much more directly, from the schools our kids attend, the condition of our roads, the quality of our water, and the safety of our communities. There are about half a million state and locally elected officials throughout the United States—but only 542 elected federal officials. And these local officials are the ones who have the power to shape our immediate communities.

Despite this, presidential or U.S. Senate elections often get much more public attention than local elections. Outside the election cycle, some Americans obsess over the latest twists and turns of Washington's political soap opera while neglecting to pay attention to what is happening in their own backyard. Some scholars have called this the "nationalization" of American politics, a phenomenon that has arisen thanks in large part to centralized news, the far reaches of social media, and the parallel decline in local news (see Action 2).[4] This interest in national politics can be a good thing but when it brings with it a sense that our lives are controlled by distant actors who know or care little about our town or neighborhood, it only compounds the declining confidence that Americans have in their government and institutions (a common trend in backsliding democracies). Conversely, polling consistently shows that Americans have more faith and trust in their local government,[5] which still gives us hope that our nation's troubling trends can be stopped and reversed—if we can get people to attend to their own community.

Local communities consist not just of local governments, but, importantly, they encompass the multitude of formal and informal ways we interact with our neighbors and share our lives with them—through schools and worship communities; shared spaces like parks, libraries, or farmers' markets; volunteer associations, local stores, businesses, and restaurants; community and sports leagues; public swimming pools or ice rinks, exercise clubs, and the like. Researchers who have studied the effectiveness of local governments and institutions have found that in communities with higher levels of civic participation, local government is more responsive than in communities with lower civic engagement.[6] Other research has shown that people who engage in their local communities—those who start the work at their front door—are more likely to work to preserve the local community's character, values, and laws.[7]

One piece of good news is that in the United States, studies have shown that working across political and ideological divisions occurs much more often in local politics and local government.[8] In fact, studies show that setting aside polarized politics to get things done occurs most often in towns with fewer than 50,000 people—a sign that our democracy is still manageable when approached via the local community.[9] Many local problems don't translate into the "left vs right" political fighting that folks see on cable TV. There's a common saying that there's no Democratic or Republican way to fill a pothole. If we set our minds to it, we could revitalize our ability to use local community to influence national politics, rather than allowing national politics to determine local community.

THE CRISIS IN OUR COMMUNITY ENGAGEMENT

Unfortunately, over the past decades, we, on the whole, have not been interacting with our neighbors as much as we used to—and this hampers our potential to work together. Rates of social and community engagement have been declining.[10] The seminal book *Bowling Alone* by sociologist Robert Putnam (first published in 2000 and updated in 2020) documents the substantial decrease in social connection experienced by Americans in the last half of the twentieth century—after a period marked by substantial levels of community engagement.[11] "We're spending time watching *Friends* as opposed to having friends," Putnam remarked in the 1990s (and what an apt 1990s-era reference it was!).[12] In the book, he posits a number of reasons for declining social connection, including the prevalence of new technologies and the changed social and political landscape near the turn of the century. But his most important insights are on social capital, the value derived from social networks that affects the health of a society and its institutions. He believed that increased social isolation would lead to undemocratic politics. Recently he has said that people can help strengthen our society through increased social interaction in our communities.

Civic engagement has continued to decline in recent years, including due to structural and systemic barriers. Approximately one in five adult Americans live in what they perceive as 'civic deserts'—a term coined by social scientists Kei Kawashima-Ginsberg and Felicia Sullivan—areas in the country where there are few opportunities to socialize in common spaces like public parks, local businesses, libraries, and places to build relationships and engage in our community.[13] According to a 2017 study, 60 percent of youth in rural areas and 30 percent of youth in urban areas perceived themselves to live in civic deserts.[14] For those living in such places, community engagement in a traditional sense is more difficult because there are fewer common spaces to facilitate connection. This can be exacerbated by limited economic resources and lack of reliable public transportation. (If you are a person in a civic desert or have loved ones in civic deserts, there are resources on ordinarypeopleaction.com on how to engage, including how you can use technology and also participate in building civic habits in your community).

Yet it isn't just structural barriers like civic deserts that have contributed to declines in community engagement across the nation. The vast majority of Americans live in places with the opportunity for social connection, but people have still become more isolated and less active in forming social bonds. To be sure, the Covid-19 pandemic accelerated this trend, but the roots were already there. Technology has made it easier and cheaper for people to access personalized entertainment in their leisure time without interacting with others, and a number of other factors (including, for many, community safety concerns) discourage people from going out into their communities. Exhaustion and overwhelm (not to mention fear and anxiety) lead to social isolation.

Interestingly, technology and the ease it brings to mass communication, while helpful in many circumstances, has also been responsible for undermining certain forms of local political action, as detailed in sociologist Theda Skocpol's book *Diminished Democracy: From Membership to Management in American Life*. Skocpol explains that social advocacy organizations that catalyzed change in the twentieth century (civil rights movement, workers' rights movement, etc.) were based on membership to local chapters where friends and colleagues would gather together in person to hold meetings and work for change. As technology evolved, many organizations focused on communicating with national masses as opposed to the often costly and time-consuming work of holding local meetings.[15] While the reach may have been broader and many have been energized and mobilized by online action, an unintended consequence of the "nationalization" of our civic and political discussions was to erode the desire for—and perceived value of—local engagement. After all, why get a babysitter for your kids and drive to a building to talk about a local issue with ten neighbors when you can join a Zoom call or an online message board to discuss "bigger" and "more important" national issues from the comfort of your laptop in your living room? To be clear, Zooms and national engagement models are incredibly important, especially now, when there are national threats to our wellbeing. Over the past year, more people across the United States have been trained in lawful nonviolent, direct action than at any point in our history because of the ability of organizers to reach large audiences online. I turn to many of these national technology-based models in my own work. Yet it is important to realize that these interactions, while critically important, cannot and do not replace local engagement. Often lost in the conversation of the national model of online political engagement is the need to strengthen the local capacity and the focus necessary to build and change our communities—we must embrace both and understand that the work for democracy, while extending across the nation, begins at our front door. At best, national organizing models include local components to support local community engagement. (In Action 5, there is a tip sheet for hosting local conversations with your community through Democracy Forward's Dinners for Democracy program, which is intended to strengthen local bonds. In Action 6, there is information on how to engage locally through the No Kings movement.)

TAKING ACTION BEGINS AT YOUR FRONT DOOR: A COMMUNITY . . . IF YOU CAN KEEP IT

It is no mistake that the nation's democratic backslide coincides with the culmination of decades of decline in civic participation and civic engagement. In the political sphere, declining community bonds and increased isolation are tools that autocratic actors use to consolidate power and further undermine democracy. When we become isolated and feel unseen, it is easy to look to the so-called strength of authoritarian rule and to forget our common bonds with one another and our collective power as "we the people." When we feel alone, we become spectators.

Declining rates of civic participation and engagement in American society have made the threats the nation faces more pronounced. The pervasive cruelty, overreach, and contempt for the rule of law that we see from President Trump and his administration have created real anxiety for many people. When combined with feelings of isolation, our collective anxiety fuels a sense of national hopelessness, which makes our fears regarding the decline in our democracy a self-fulfilling prophecy. We face a perfect storm of democratic decline, but one we can weather together with fortitude and a shared commitment to restoring our democracy, which begins right at our front door.

As we've seen over the past year with the president's attempt to militarize our cities, our best defense against encroaching autocracy is community organizing and mutual aid. In sub-zero temperatures, thousands of community members came together in Minnesota to support one another in opposing ICE raids and violence by our own government on the streets of Minneapolis. And, in areas that have been decimated by natural disasters, communities are rebuilding together. Working with others at the local level to solve a problem can help us find the power we need to demand bigger changes for our society and to "buy into" a common good that serves all of us. This type of common purpose is central to the ability of our democracy to thrive, but we don't need to wait for our close community to come under attack to get started. In fact, we *cannot* wait; we must urgently take action. The following six steps provide ways to get started.

SIX STEPS FOR TAKING ACTION AT YOUR FRONT DOOR

1. Get to know your community. The first step to strengthening our local community muscle is to take a hard look at how engaged you are personally. How can you change your habits and practices to be more connected to those around you? If you have become disconnected to your community (or have never been connected), there is no shame in that—modern life has made it difficult, which is partly why we are in this mess! What matters now is that you go out your front door and engage. It may feel difficult at first to make time; schedules get busy, you feel pulled in a number of different directions, and it's easier to follow usual routines. Remember that there is no one "right way" to engage. The chart below provides some basic steps you can take to begin to get local or to deepen your engagement with your local community. They all help enhance the strength of our communities—and our democracy as a whole. But first you need to open your front door.

Take a Day (5 to 6 Hours) to Begin Getting Local

CONNECT WITH YOUR COMMUNITY

These can also be broken up into smaller tasks over the course of several days

➔ **Get to know your neighbors.** They are your support group, and you are theirs. They may live in the same apartment building, even on the same floor as you, in the house next door, on the same street, or further afield. How many of them do you know? Do you wave at them and ask about their day? Think about ways that you can interact with them more. Consider starting local potlucks or block parties, or movie nights. If you live in a community where this is not possible, what else could you do?

➔ **Support your local library and make sure you have a library card.** Libraries are essential to communities, providing access to computers and internet, connecting people to local resources, as well as lending books and movies. Consider joining a library group on a topic that interests you or signing up for a community lecture. If you live in an area that does not have a public library, you can usually become a member at a nearby library with proof of address. (And perhaps helping your community get a library is a local action to consider!) You can also explore online and digital libraries. This is a great thing to do with kids and young people too.

→ **Identify the sources for local news (newspapers, blogs, television, radio) in your community and learn about ways you can be supportive of their work.** Subscriptions to local news sources are often very affordable, will help you stay engaged with their local reporting, and help fund their essential services. Find out if you have a public radio or television station in your community. Sign up for their newsletter. Identify ways you can support them, even if it is just listening or being informed. Call the local station and offer feedback! You'd be surprised how rarely this happens. They really do listen to customer comments and perspectives.

→ **If you are religious and attend a center of worship, try to know more about fellow congregants.** Do members of your church/temple/mosque engage with others in the community? Could you get involved with community outreach or events with them?

→ **Your area may have public spaces for the community; a local, state, or national park, a town square—find, know, and visit them.** Understand the challenges these spaces face in surviving and being used to promote community engagement.

→ **Learn your community's significant cultural spaces.** Does your community have a museum or a gallery or maybe a concert hall? Find them, know them. Make a list of ones you may wish to frequent and support.

→ **Make a plan to frequent local small businesses and farmers' or artisan markets,** if your community has them. You might also explore your local chamber of commerce or business associations.

→ **Make sure you know your local polling place** (see vote.org) and the timing of upcoming elections.

→ **Find out more about your local public transit.** If you don't usually use public transportation, understand how to use it and how it can be improved to facilitate community engagement and connect neighborhoods and their residents.

→ **Look for the helpers.** What are the service organizations in your community that are making a difference? Where is your local food pantry, job training program, homeless shelter? Who is helping immigrants? Make a list of organizations to explore. Determine one or two organizations to keep up with and consider supporting or volunteering. At a minimum, sign up for alerts and newsletters and be informed. This is another great task to do with kids or young people.

→ **Join something fun!** This could be a club that matches an interest of yours, such as running, golfing, birdwatching, knitting, or playing board/card games. Instead of occasional activities with friends, maybe set up a standing evening at a local restaurant or venue.

→ **Get engaged in local organizations such as those that focus on charity and volunteer work to help those in need.** Consider coaching or volunteering to assist with youth sports leagues. Look for your people. If you live in a place where you feel as if you don't belong, it is important to find your people and engage together. This may take more intentionality, but they are there and need you too. More on this in Action 4 (page 109) and Action 5 (page 132).

Working through these steps, you should end up with lists of places and organizations to explore, community connections to make, and needs that exist in your community. These observations can be touchpoints for action and for engagement—when combined with the steps from Action 1, they provide a good blueprint for where to get started.

2. Commit to community involvement. Community engagement and social bonds are about habits and consistency—and even small actions make a big difference. Take an inventory of community groups you can connect with, things you can do, and ways you can engage. Identify one or two small actions you will commit to taking. You may already be taking these actions and, if so, recommit or add to them. Make sure that each action can be repeated at least once a month so that you are working on establishing the habit of consistent engagement. These types of actions might involve volunteering at the local school, engaging with others who attend religious services, interacting with people who receive support services, visiting your library, dropping off food or donations to a pantry, picking up trash as part of a cleanup program, coaching a youth team, escorting people into reproductive healthcare clinics, or tutoring adults or kids. You might want to become a regular attendee of a community band or book group. If you lean into community involvement with a friend, you'll hold each other accountable. If you are a parent or live with young people, set similar expectations for them. Additional ideas are available at ordinarypeopleaction.com.

Start 'Em Young

Local community engagement is for everyone. There are a number of ways to partner with your kids or young people in your life to act and strengthen community. These steps also build confidence and leadership habits. You can find more information at ordinarypeopleaction.com.

→ ***For kids.*** The best way to encourage civic engagement is to involve your kids in their community. Using the public library, visiting local parks, getting to know small businesses in your area all build civic muscle. Talk with your kids about why their community matters. As children get older, help them develop service-based habits. Consider taking them to volunteer at a community garden, their school, or a local drive for the community. Even lending a hand to a neighbor can be important. Serving others builds confidence and leadership skills, in addition to being a good thing for the community. Talk with kids about the importance of fostering solidarity within their own community and with others across the nation and how they can engage as communities come under threat in this time.

→ ***For teens.*** In addition to direct volunteer and community service efforts, encourage teens to approach problems they encounter with an "agent" mindset, as discussed in Action 1. Teens can practice organizing collective action to bring about changes in their schools or in other community settings (sports teams, clubs). Encourage teens to become interested in politics and social movements and help facilitate their participation. This can involve supporting teens in researching and creating accurate content on particular local or national issues, using their phones to serve as citizen journalists, supporting or making art, understanding worker power and unions, and more. As noted on page 50, The Civics Center has excellent resources on student-led voter registration drives, which helps increase younger voter participation and builds organizing and important civic skills.

3. Engage with local government civic institutions and find ways to be more civically active. What happens in your city council, school board, local courthouse, and library board meetings matter. It matters to your community, and it also matters to our democracy. Who you elect to represent you at the state and local level matters—and who represents your local community in Congress also matters. The chart that follows includes some steps you can take to learn more about ways to be more civically active.

Find More Ways to be Civically Active

Further information on all of the below can be found at ordinarypeopleaction.com.

→ **Explore your local government.** Get information on your city or town hall, local officials, and their hours of availability. (If you need assistance finding your local government, you can log on to usa.gov/local-governments.) Learn how to find out when city council or other public meetings are scheduled and mark one on your calendar to attend virtually or in person.

→ **Get to know your local leaders.** Learn who represents you at the local and state levels and research their positions on different issues, from public school funding to community safety and environmental health. This includes your state and national representatives, school board members, city councilperson, sheriff, local judges, and more. If your local leaders are promoting the well-being of your community and are committed to our democracy, find ways to support them. If they are not, make your views and expectations known to them. You might wish to consider running for a position yourself or encouraging others to run.

→ **Get smart on your local schools (even if you don't have kids).** Consider attending school board meetings. Stay informed on issues affecting your local schools—and if you aren't satisfied, find ways to engage. Support someone in running for the school board (or run yourself). If your schools need additional funding, learn more about how to advocate for that at the state and federal levels as well as local options like supporting bond initiatives. You can also create or support local education foundations where private community members donate to support public schools.

→ **Don't forget your local courts.** Local courts handle a range of matters that affect the everyday lives of people—from child custody issues to leasing and business transactions to landlord-tenant disputes to holding those who break the law accountable. In many communities, judges are elected, so you should learn about your judges' record of service.

→ **Vote in local elections.** As discussed in Action 1, make sure you are registered to vote and have a plan for voting.

4. Protect your neighbors. In many places across the nation, our families, neighbors, and communities are being attacked by the very government that should be serving all of us. This assault should not be normalized—it is part of the broader democratic backslide. ICE has raided neighborhoods, schools, businesses, and homes—grabbing people, parents, even kids, disrupting families and spreading fear. Children come home from school not knowing if their parents will be there still. Countless warrantless arrests are taking place; homes are being barged into by law enforcement. The national guard is present in many communities (including where I am raising my son), because the president is seeking to militarize our cities. Hate-based violence is increasing across the nation, while the gun violence epidemic threatens all of us—from our schools to community spaces.

These events make everyone feel unsafe and can lead to terror and trauma for many. Some of you may be experiencing these events yourself and others may be seeing the impact on loved ones, neighbors, or community members. Some of you may be no stranger to experiencing terror and violence from people in power. These times, though unprecedented in many regards, are not new for many people in Black and Brown communities in our country. Whether or not it's happening directly to you, however, it takes all of us working together to make change happen. Now is not the time to sit by. Now is the time to make a commitment to our families, our neighbors, and our communities to protect one another. We need to be our neighbors' keepers.

The power and resilience of local communities have been seen across the nation in response to the government's actions—from people peacefully mobilizing in the streets in the millions to communities protecting neighbors from arrests to citizens documenting harmful and illegal acts perpetrated before their very eyes in their hometowns. We can all seek to ensure that the basic dignity of our neighbors is protected—and that the government operates to serve the people, not terrorize them.

The box below provides some simple steps we can take to protect ourselves and our neighbors—understanding that every community has its unique attributes and that we all come to this from unique places and ways of engaging.

Act Now, Prepare Now: Protecting Your Neighbors and Community Members

Visit ordinarypeopleaction.com for more information and resources.

→ **Know your rights.** Start by knowing your rights and the rights of people in your community. This includes the right to require that law enforcement officers, including ICE agents, have a judicial warrant (signed by a judge) before entering one's home; the right to remain silent; the right to ask for a lawyer; and the right to say that you do not consent to what is happening to you. It also includes the right of bystanders in many states to document and record and peacefully voice information about the rights of their neighbors on the streets.

→ **Make a plan.** Talk with your loved ones (including your children) and make a plan for what to do if your community experiences disruptive activity from federal or state agents or other law enforcement. This may include (1) gathering your documentation, making copies, and making sure a loved one or neighbor has your information. If your neighbors are at risk, offer to be part of their plan of documenting their rights, assisting their families and loved ones in navigating the situation, and ensuring that people have the representation they need. While there is no legal requirement for U.S. citizens to carry documents to prove citizenship, having your documents in order could be helpful, especially for those who are legal permanent residents or noncitizens who have a recognized legal right to be in the United States; (2) exploring where you may call for legal services if you or your neighbor are targeted or detained; (3) planning for what you may want to have with you at all times, like a phone that can record or an index card with important phone numbers; and (4) watching and learning from communities across the nation and partnering with your local community to makes these plans together.

→ **Offer help and work in partnership.** Make sure your neighbors and community members know what you can offer them if they are in need. Can you provide a communal meal once a week? Can you provide legal resources or research? Rides or help with negotiating public transportation? Childcare? Donations? Can you provide jobs for people or financial assistance? Can you provide computer access or language translation services? What can you do to encourage equitable law enforcement practices? Consider joining group chats and Signal text chains to protect your neighbors and using your technology to document what is happening around you.

→ **Understand the role of local law enforcement.** In many communities across the nation, local law enforcement has been caught between meeting the needs of the community and the pressure of federal enforcement. In some communities, local law enforcement has aided and abetted the violation of people's constitutional rights—with federal courts finding the actions of both local law enforcement and ICE unconstitutional. In some communities, excessive force and police brutality are not new. In other local areas, local law enforcement has been able to partner with communities to ensure their rights are protected within the bounds of the law. It is important to be vigilant to understand the role of local and state law enforcement in your community. Understand if your community benefits from community and equitable policing and law enforcement models—and if your local law enforcement is likely to help protect your community during federal raids—or if the record of your community law enforcement is concerning. The Center for Policing Equity has put together good questions to help you investigate your local law enforcement's practices. You can access those questions by visiting policingequity.org/community-how-to-guide-undercovering-your-law-enforcement-agencys-interactions-with-ice/.

➔ **Communicate and document.** Many neighborhoods and communities are communicating through message apps and other platforms about the state of their community, what is happening, and how one can help. Join these groups. Understand how to document what is happening in your community through making recordings, talking with journalists, or writing.

➔ **Donate.** If you are able, set up recurring monthly donations to trusted organizations that challenge unlawful policies, provide legal defense, and help the people targeted navigate the legal system (including providing bond funds).

- → **Advocate.** Don't forget to advocate for your neighbors and community members. Show up to peaceful protests and demonstrations. These matter. If protesting isn't your thing, use other resources to advocate for your community with local, state, and national leaders. Use your cell phone and take action through 5 Calls (5calls.org) to make a local impact.

- → **Organize and engage.** Local chapters of a number of national and regional organizations are revitalizing as the visibility of the needs of communities are on the rise. Groups like Indivisible, the American Civil Liberties Union (ACLU), and the National Association for the Advancement of Colored People (NAACP) are organizing millions at the local level. You may wish to find a local chapter of an organization that is focused on protecting the rights of people or on advocating for specific policies and changes within your community. See if you can volunteer or offer practical support to an organization you think is doing good work in your community. Democracy Forward has built ways to help you engage with your own personal community and expand the actions being taken there. Participate in local strikes or boycotts in your community if it is needed to resist violence by the government.

- → **Connect the dots.** It is important to connect the dots of what is happening in our communities that lead to the elected governmental leaders who are causing direct harm or not doing enough to stop those who are. Part of our work in protecting our neighbors is to ensure we are politically engaged, demanding more of our elected representatives, and using our power to vote.

5. Understand your position and your privilege. Right now in our nation all communities are at risk, but our position and privilege determine our level of risk as well as our considerations for taking action. For example, there is a demonstrated pattern of law enforcement targeting or profiling Black and Brown, Indigenous, immigrant, and other communities of color. This means that the risk and safety calculus for communities of color is different than white communities. The Trump-Vance administration and many of their allies (including at the state and local level) have targeted LGBTQ people and non-binary people. This means the risk and safety calculus for these community members may be different than that of cisgender, heterosexual people. There is also rampant discrimination based on how people worship—with Jews, Muslims, and people who practice other minority religions often the subjects of expressions of hate. Limited access to financial resources can also affect one's safety and security. If you are in a relatively more privileged position because of your race, sex, wealth, education, and/or other personal characteristics, you should consider if there are ways to leverage that position and privilege for people and communities who do not share this same privilege. Too often, those who are most at risk have to do the frontline work of fighting for liberation. Those with privilege should acknowledge this reality and also be willing to do the frontline work. Our liberation—our fight for freedom—is a collective endeavor. That is what this book is about: ensuring that everyone can find a way to engage in their community as it fits their circumstances.

6. Keep your dollars local. You may have heard of voting with your dollars, and perhaps you participate in consumer boycotts, but giving back to your community includes choosing your local grocery store, driving an extra five minutes to pick up burgers at the locally owned joint instead of the global chain, or buying holiday and birthday presents at a nearby small business. Focusing on keeping your money in your community as much as possible helps to fortify community resources and supports those closest to the work and ensures that necessary services are provided.

A Republic . . . If You Can Keep It

There is an often-told story of what happened when Benjamin Franklin left the Constitutional Convention in Philadelphia in 1787. The Constitution was controversial, and many were concerned that the ratification of the Constitution would create too much centralized power. Franklin was asked, "What have we got, a republic or a monarchy?" Franklin responded, "A republic, if you can keep it."[16] His words were not directed to elected leaders, rather it was a charge to the people. ***If YOU can keep it.*** Franklin's words ring true today. The work to keep our republic rests on ordinary people staying engaged and finding their collective power. A commitment to our republic is still vibrant and meaningful in our local communities and can be the wellspring for a renewal.

ACTION 4

Practice Tailgate Accountability

"MY WIFE WAS AT THE INSURRECTION," boasted a man in a nice suit with a red MAGA wrist band as we sat in the gallery of the U.S. House of Representatives just weeks after President Trump was inaugurated. We were both there to listen to the president's address to a joint session of Congress. It was only March, but the president and Elon Musk had already unlawfully taken a chainsaw to congressionally authorized government programs and begun firing the civil servant employees of the federal government. Since the late 1800s, in order to minimize corruption, civil servants have not been appointed to their positions based on political affiliation or loyalty to a particular president or ideological agenda; instead, they are hired for their merit, swear an oath to the Constitution, and work from administration to administration regardless of whether the president is a Republican or a Democrat. Most Americans (92 percent) believe that civil servants should be hired in this way, based on merit, not political loyalty.[1] President Trump does not agree.

Instead, President Trump was adhering to the agenda outlined in the Heritage Foundation's Project 2025, a radical right-wing blueprint for taking a wrecking ball to the government. He was decimating congressionally authorized federal agencies and indiscriminately firing career civil servants to replace them with (often unqualified) partisan loyalists. Even as we can acknowledge that the government isn't perfect, or as efficient as we want, it becomes far *less* efficient and *more* corrupt when those who work for the government are hired based on political loyalty rather than ability. Within weeks, the effects of these rash actions were felt around the world. Carefully negotiated diplomatic initiatives—from trade and arms agreements to climate agreements—were abandoned. Decades of work to address the causes of climate catastrophes were lost as meteorologists were fired and weather forecast programs shuttered. Warehouses of food rotted instead of reaching hungry people in the poorest parts of the world—and contracts to purchase vast sums of American farmers' harvests to feed others were canceled. The Trump administration even dismissed nuclear scientists before realizing their critical role in national security and recalling them in a panic.

Our Democracy Forward team heard from civil servants who had been summarily fired despite their years of patriotic service, as well as from people from all parts of the American landscape who had been hurt by these unprecedented budget cuts and firings, who reached out to see if anything could be done to stop the wreckage. We knew there was no congressional authority for Trump's orders, so our team sprang into action, launching a number of lawsuits on behalf of these workers and harmed citizens.

I was at the joint session of Congress as a guest of Senator Chris Van Hollen of Maryland, who had invited me as a symbol of support for our nation's civil servants. Sitting in the gallery, among a multitude of people—Republicans, Independents, and

Democrats—who were there to hear the president's speech, I introduced myself to the person next to me. As we made small talk, I learned that he was from my home state of Texas and soon we were chatting about the places and foods that we both liked there. After several minutes of conversation, he told me that he was an ally of the president and how proud he was that his wife had come to the Capitol on January 6, 2021. He must have assumed that I was there as an ally of the president too. I probably look like many of the women with whom he was used to socializing—I still keep my hair full like many women from Texas do ("the higher the hair, the closer to God," as the women at the salon I went to growing up used to say), and I wear pearls in formal settings even when they aren't in vogue.

As I looked at him, he quickly realized he was wrong in his assumption. "We're here for different reasons," I said with a smile, but in a more direct tone than I had used when we were discussing barbecue. When he asked what I meant, I explained that I had been invited to the speech because I led a team that was suing the president's administration for the harm done to people across the nation. I told him that I thought it was important that everyone has access to a lawyer and that people are able to defend their rights when the government violates them. I also told him that I was profoundly horrified by the events of January 6, knew people who were put in danger that day, and continued to mourn those who were killed by the violent rioters seeking to undermine the 2020 U.S. presidential election.

He seemed shocked by my direct but polite tone, but he also seemed to appreciate my honesty. We continued to engage in conversation, heated at times, on various issues. I challenged his statements and assertions—and he responded in kind to things I said. We even found alignment on several issues. Throughout, I was firm in my views and didn't mince words, including the irony that those who supported the January 6 insurrection were sitting in the very Capitol that they had violently assaulted.

At the end of the speech, he looked at me and said something to the effect of, "You know, I would have never known you were invited here by a Democrat. Heck, you are one of the only Democrats that I've ever talked to . . . and you are pretty nice." I too was a little shocked at how we had managed to stay in conversation despite our differences. This chapter is about how to have those conversations, how to try to talk across our differences, to remind ourselves about what we have in common.

Like this gentleman, many Americans no longer have real-world interaction with those outside their own political bubble—and that can contribute to a polarized society. Syracuse University political science professor Johanna Dunaway has studied Americans' beliefs about political polarization and found that deep divisions have arisen when partisan media ecosystems encourage people to assume the worst about those who are members of a political party that is not their own.[2] Recent polling from the Pew Research Center reports a substantial rise in partisan hostility with 72 percent of Republicans and 63 percent of Democrats viewing the opposing party as immoral, a significant increase since 2016 when 47 percent and 35 percent, respectively, held these views.[3] We no longer just disagree with our political opponents; we actively dislike or distrust them. We view our political parties not just as associations of people with common beliefs but as a deeply rooted identity, similar to our allegiance to a sports team.

Unfortunately, this discord is getting in the way of fighting for our freedom and rebuilding the promise of our democracy. As authoritarian actions by the second Trump administration accelerate, we are wasting time, energy, and attention on fighting one another—which, of course, is what leaders with autocratic tendencies most want. In order to move toward one another rather than further apart and learn to work together, we must gain a better understanding of the divisions we are seeing in the United States. This begins with understanding how polarization operates in political and social systems—and what it means when people say the United States is a "divided" nation. Only then can we hope to begin the work of overcoming these divisions and put into practice what I call "tailgate accountability"—listening to people who may believe differently than us, accepting our personal responsibility for deescalating polarization, and taking it upon ourselves to hold others in our communities accountable for their contributions.

UNDERSTANDING POLARIZATION

Rulers who are seeking to consolidate power—whether monarchs, aristocrats, dictators, or autocrats—understand that "divide and conquer" is a useful tactic to control populations. Pitting people against one another can keep their focus off a leader's failures or their autocratic agenda. As discussed in Action 1, we are seeing democratically elected leaders across the globe exploit weaknesses in their respective governments' checks and balances systems to increase and consolidate their power.

In order to polarize people, autocratic political movements often seek scapegoats to vilify. This tactic creates an "us versus them" mentality as people band together against the maligned "other" and rally behind the leader who is saving them from that "other." The Nazis vilified Jews, Poles, and immigrants in the 1930s. White southerners in the U.S. used degrading stereotypes about Black people to justify segregation. Today, Russia's Vladimir Putin blames his political and economic failures on an invisible column of outside agitators from the United States and Europe, claiming that they were sent to weaken Russia. Ironically, he uses his "foreign meddling" narrative as justification to do his own meddling in U.S. politics. The U.S. Senate has released multiple reports concluding that Russian intelligence has targeted African Americans and other populations in the United States to inflame U.S. political polarization. For Putin, a divided America is weak and easier to exploit.[4] President Trump's actions mimic these tactics. For years he demanded the first Black president to present his citizenship papers and continues to label immigrants as criminals. These targeted racist attacks are aimed at dividing people to consolidate his own power.

SCAPEGOATING AND STEREOTYPING IN THE UNITED STATES

The harmful political scapegoating and polarization that has befallen other backsliding democracies are also present in our politics. While effective politicians—from the left and the right—often rely on messaging that identifies problems and promises solutions, President Trump's MAGA movement seeks to frame systemic and structural problems, such as job loss and economic downturn, in personal terms, shifting the blame to specific groups of people—especially immigrants and non-whites. President Trump and the MAGA movement have found this type of scapegoating incredibly effective in gaining support and spreading division. Sadly, researchers have noted that people prefer this kind of personal narrative, finding it more satisfying to have someone to blame for their misfortune than to accept that they are worse off economically because of systemic policy failures or structural barriers. In the 2024 presidential election, the Republican party spent more than $247 million on advertisements denigrating immigrants and more than $215 million on others that maligned trans people.[5] Those who supported these ads and similar ones called them "wildly successful" in helping to deliver the election for President Trump and aligned Republicans.[6]

Since resuming office, Trump has continued to rely on the tactic of scapegoating others to attempt to consolidate his power and build support, routinely calling out different groups—immigrants, political opponents, the press—as the source of the country's problems with the suggestion that only he can provide solutions and restore order. To justify the targeting he has referred to people from Somalia as "garbage," and people in his administration call immigrants "dogs." White House and official government websites routinely depict racist tropes and images—from images of Brown men behind bars with "wanted" signs to images likening our former president and first lady to apes. Peaceful protesters are referred to as domestic terrorists. Rather than unite the American people against a common enemy or behind a unified vision, the president has suggested that leaders of the Democratic Party are "enemies of the people" who should be arrested and even executed. Republican officials and the president's surrogates simply laugh off his comments as political theater when asked about them on nightly TV talk shows, insinuating that such language and threats do not have real world impact. Unfortunately, the rise in political violence in America and the increasingly hardline views of his followers alarmingly suggest that some people do not believe the president is joking.

AMERICANS ACTUALLY ALIGN ON MANY ISSUES

Despite partisan vitriol and the feeling many have that America is impossibly divided, we still have a lot more in common with one another than the media, which thrives on conflict, would have us believe. (Remember, as we noted in Action 2, that sensationalism gains our attention more than neutral reporting and drives advertising dollars.) Rachel Kleinfeld of the Carnegie Endowment of International Peace has noted that "Americans across parties share many policy preferences," including on contentious issues such as abortion and how to teach U.S. history.[7] During the 2024 election, moderates, liberals, and conservatives all expressed disagreement with proposals outlined in the Heritage Foundation's Project 2025, from dismantling the Department of Education to canceling core community programs.[8] Indeed, Project 2025 became such a toxic brand that Trump was forced to disavow any association with it on the campaign trail. (Of course, once in office, he has steadily implemented many of the project's unpopular initiatives—he simply avoids use of the name Project 2025.)[9]

Ironically, research suggests that the deepest divisions actually occur between politicians, whether through a misunderstanding of the other party's positions or a desire to leverage sensationalism to promote their own brand. The political stage offers a dramatized, hyper-polarized impression of where the people in the country stand on core issues. Such hyping of the differences between the constituents of the two political parties prevents progress. The result is that many people disengage in politics because they are told that the other side is opposed to everything they believe. In the 2024 U.S. presidential election 90 million people eligible to vote sat out the election, which is more people than those who voted for either Trump or Harris.[10] While this is troubling, the good news is that there is an opportunity for most Americans to take a deep breath and realize that much more unites us than divides us. Our values and ideological rifts are not as vast as our always-angry media ecosystems and politicians insist they are.

In rich irony, those across the ideological spectrum today *actu-*

ally agree on certain policy issues, yet people are *angrier* at their opposing political party than they have been in the past. For example, according to a Gallup poll from 2025, the vast majority of Americans oppose political violence, believe the United States is a stronger nation because of our diversity, and support capping the money wealthy individuals and corporations can spend in political races.[11] Yet when it comes to getting things done in government, gridlock between the political parties prevents progress. In some ways, political parties have become like sports teams—to which people remain loyal regardless of what that party does, instead of judging political parties and politicians on issues and actions.

HOW DO WE REDUCE POLARIZATION WHILE STAYING TRUE TO OUR VALUES?

In order to stop the cycle of political polarization, the first step we can take is being self-aware about our own place in a political ecosystem and the groups of people we consider—even subconsciously—our political "enemy." The chances are high that anyone we might regard as a political opponent is someone with whom we don't engage frequently in our daily life. Civil rights lawyer Bryan Stevenson champions the notion of "proximity," emphasizing that genuine change (and understanding) comes from being physically close with those who are struggling or marginalized.[12] By contrast, making judgments from a distance runs the risk of making harmful assumptions and supporting political actions that directly target others as causing harm to us. In the context Stevenson writes about—he works with incarcerated and impoverished populations—he argues that proximity can rewrite entrenched cultural narratives about poverty and deservedness. This expanded sense of understanding can enable better policy making in which solutions are sought that do not dehumanize our fellow Americans.

This concept of proximity has held true in other contexts. As people in the nation started being in community with openly LGBTQ people, acceptance grew. Assumptions were replaced by real experiences in which the stereotypes were disproven. It is easy to hate or generalize about an acronym—but it is hard to hate someone who is your neighbor, your daughter, your colleague, or your friend.

In our nation, the president and his allies (including at the state and local levels) need us to participate in the us-versus-them mentality in order to consolidate their power. Being willing to consider that those we call "them" are more like us than we think is an important act of resistance ordinary people can make. Seeking to find this common humanity is a threat to those who want to "divide and conquer," meaning that finding our community in those we may consider "other than" or "different from" us is a powerful step in fighting for our freedom. This work is crucial on a political level too. We must deeply question claims that we, as a people, are divided (people are not as divided on issues as those who seek to polarize us want us to believe) and continually seek to evaluate our beliefs about people who may seem politically different from us. We need to stop making assumptions and start digging in.

COMBATING POLARIZATION WITH TAILGATE ACCOUNTABILITY

Despite the lure of Friday night lights in Texas, I didn't grow up routinely going to sporting events. I was raised in an all-female home with my mother and sister, and, for us, that meant we didn't routinely attend live sports events. By contrast, my husband has been a football fan his whole life. As I began spending weekends with his family and friends, I learned that going to sporting events—whether football or other games—was more fun than I expected it would be. The competition, the drama between teams, and the overall energy that comes with live sports pulled me in. But what I really learned to love was the tailgate, the pre-game party. All kinds of people getting together outdoors, grilling food or sharing drinks, kids running around, and music playing.

After college graduation, tailgates became a way to reconnect with friends we would never otherwise see because of schedules or the distance we live from one another. Tailgates also allowed me to get to know people I would never have otherwise met—people who may have very little in common with me politically, but who have gathered to watch the same team and participate in the same game-day rituals. I enjoyed these bonding moments so much that my husband and I began to find other ways to tailgate before games, even when we could not be at the stadium in person—such as inviting other fans over for at-home tailgates or visiting a sports bar where a game is on.

For me, being around people who may not agree with me on all social and political issues is not new. I grew up in a community in central Texas that tends to be conservative and many of my friends did not see eye to eye with me on a lot of issues. Nevertheless, we learned to live and laugh together, to support one another, and, ultimately, to want the best for one another. As I've gone to various tailgates over the years, I've connected with new people who likely don't agree with me on all issues or who may see themselves as on a different part of the political spectrum than me. Yet, when we talk at the tailgate, we have a lot in common: We want our kids to have what they need; we want a good job; we want to be safe and healthy; we're stressed about the holidays or upcoming events; and, of course, we want our team to win.

I think about all the potential friendships that I would have missed out on over the years if I had seen these tailgate goers (many of whom are now friends) as opponents, rather than our teammates; how lonely and boring those tailgates would have been if I had refused to speak to someone because I knew they differed from me politically. And I think about how much getting to know them challenged what I was told about them by the media and politicians seeking to foster polarization.

I also think about the close-knit groups of loved ones torn apart by conflicts about politics. Families who have a difficult time spending holidays together because of visceral disagreements. Friends who become disconnected.

Practicing tailgate accountability involves us getting out of our echo chambers. It involves approaching others with a sense of curiosity, while recognizing our commonality and acknowledging not everyone will agree with our perspective. It requires holding our communities and ourselves accountable for making assumptions about the "other." When we do this, we create opportunities to learn more about those around us and to break down barriers that serve the interest of those in power who seek to divide us. Practicing tailgate accountability means affirming the humanity of all people and asking the same from one another. It is one way we can reclaim our power and strengthen our collective agency. The purpose of tailgate accountability is not to win someone over to your side—in the same way that when Cowboys fans play the Packers at a sports pub, we don't try to convert each other. The purpose is to break down our impressions of the "other" to minimize polarization. Let's take a look at what this requires in practice.

SEVEN STEPS OF PRACTICING TAILGATE ACCOUNTABILITY

First, find your tailgate. Where do you go in your life where you interact with people who may not believe all the same ideas or identify the same way you do? Maybe it's an activity you participate in. Or your faith community or an organization you belong to. Your place of work or the gym? At actual tailgates or sporting events? Your neighborhood bar? Family events? Once you've identified what serves as a tailgate (or tailgates) for you, make a mental note.

If you find that your tailgate doesn't come to mind easily, then practicing tailgate accountability starts with reflecting on how to change that. Make a commitment to get out of your comfort zone and discover ways to get to know people who may have different commitments or beliefs than you, but who may have something in common with you (maybe they are a fan of the same sports team or enjoy the same gym you like). Strive to not be like the guy at the joint session of Congress I sat next to, who claimed to not know anyone from the opposite political party.

Second, focus on the person, not their politics. Build a relationship with those who are different from you and genuinely get to know them without a political focus. What connections do you share? Do you both care for the same person? Are you part of the same neighborhood; do you both enjoy the same hobby? Do you volunteer or work at the same place? Do you like the same sports team, TV shows, books? Building a relationship based on common interests is helpful to establishing trust and reminding all of us of our common humanity.

Third, explore common ground. As you build the relationship, get to know areas where you believe there is common ground (or potential common ground) on social, political, and values issues. Explore those areas within and apart from politics. Do you both care about the quality of school that your kids attend? Do you both care about healthcare costs and grocery prices? Are things happening in your community that concern you both?

Fourth, get the facts. When political issues do eventually arise, try to keep the conversation as a joint exploration for common ground as much as possible. Avoid generalizations and acknowledge the limitations of your perspective. Seek to have a conversation about issues or politics focused on understanding, not a cable-television style debate. Be sure to have the facts and bring them into the conversation, but don't use facts to silence the other person. Use and cite sources to help validate what you are saying and to build trust with the person you are speaking with. Having the facts shows the other person that you respect them enough to research and come prepared. They will also come with facts, so extend the same respect to them. When you do not know something, readily acknowledge your limitation. Don't be afraid to show vulnerability.

Too often, people have a set of refrains, soundbites, or talking points they find compelling and think can be deployed to effectively dismantle their opponent's political position. (I like to imagine some of my relatives who keep political news channels on all day, memorizing their favorite "gotcha" zingers.) Remember, the purpose of the conversations in tailgate accountability is to share information, not to try to convince someone of your world view. This is because for most of us—whether we realize it or not—our opinions and values are part of a larger psychologically complex political identity that doesn't change easily. (A Packers fan is not going to immediately switch to rooting for the Cowboys.) The process of change is a slow alchemy that allows new ideas and values to seep into someone's perspective and, only over time, may alter their politics incrementally. A "frontal assault" of partisan debate talking points is more likely to sour whatever nascent relationship you have built and prompt your friend to put on their "political armor" and reply with their own partisan barbs, shutting down the part of the brain that was seeking connection and shared values.

Data continues to show that when people discuss specifics as opposed to generalities, they can come closer together and have more productive conversations.[13] This is especially true in a polarized environment that can encourage scapegoating. In discussing a political issue, frame your discussion as an issue bigger than both of you, rather than a sales pitch to change their mind. Remember in these discussions, you are not on the floor of Congress, and you aren't going to be voting on legislation at the end of your discussion. So, there's no pressure. Be curious, and ready to learn.

Fifth, choose being heard over being right. When speaking with someone who may not have the same background or agree with you on an issue, your goal should be to melt a little bit of the ice between you, not sledgehammer a chunk off. What that means is that sometimes we need to be careful with our word choices so that we are communicating in a way the other person can hear with an open mind. Remember, your goal is not to change someone's mind. Your goal is to work to find a place of common humanity that reduces polarization and to correct assumptions the other person may make about you or your political beliefs and the assumptions you have about them. And as much as you seek to be heard, it's also your job to hear them out. Respect and common ground are far more important than bulldozing and self-righteousness. I have some friends who have confessed to me that they don't want to engage with others or find common ground because of how deeply hurt they are by the positions people take. This is understandable (and, as discussed below, it is important to have boundaries in these conversations or in deciding to have a conversation at all; the purpose of tailgate accountability is not to participate in conversations that may harm or subject you or your loved ones to hate). Yet for us to really break the cycle of polarization in America—a cycle that is being driven by those who wish to take away our freedom by dividing us—we have to take some steps to reach beyond our comfortable circles.

Talking at the Tailgate

TIPS AND PHRASES TO KEEP THE CONVERSATION PRODUCTIVE

➔ **Acknowledge common emotions.** "I understand that you are afraid." "I understand that you feel unseen." "I hear you." "I understand that when people say ___, it makes you feel ___." "I am so sorry to hear that ___ happened to you, and I'm sure it impacts the way you see ___ issue." "I know how upsetting/horrifying it is that the government . . ."

➔ **Affirm the person, not the politics.** "I understand that you believe this. I don't agree with that, but I respect you and appreciate you sharing your views with me." "I know your heart and know that you believe this is the right thing. I do not agree with you, but I want you to know I appreciate understanding your views."

➔ **Affirm common values (where they exist).** "We both value the future for our kids." "We both want people to be safe." "We both believe that all people should be viewed equally by their government." "We both have a deep concern for the future and want future generations to have more than we did."

→ **Don't shy away from your values.** "In the same way I am showing you respect, you need to understand that I feel strongly about ___ (insert your values and beliefs). I will listen to you and have an open mind, but I do want you to know where I am coming from."

Sixth, set and enforce boundaries. There will be circumstances when it is not ideal for you to engage with someone at all. Building bridges across political differences does not mean being open to the views of someone who refuses to acknowledge your humanity, your right to exist, or your rights to equality. Self-care and self-preservation mean that you do not have to (and should not) engage with people who want to harm you or your loved ones. This includes friends and acquaintances, the general public, or in family settings. Family conversations can be difficult, especially since there are often heightened emotions and power dynamics at play. No one—whether a member of the public, your community, or a member of your family—has the right to subject you to hate and demonization. So don't feel compelled to have conversations with people who deny your or your loved ones' humanity or who undermine your existence.

If you end up in such a conversation and the conversation moves to an unproductive or harmful place, say so, and discontinue the exchange firmly but politely. There is no need to spend hours rehashing an issue, especially if you are feeling vulnerable or unsafe. Simply stating, "Your comment is inconsistent with my values. We do not have to discuss it further, but you should know, we do not agree," is a good way to express your boundary and encourage accountability. In Action 6, we will discuss some tips for building and practicing the courage that this requires.

Seventh, understand how the steps work together. You may sense some inherent tension between the notion of getting to know and having relationships with people who may have strongly different views than you and also enforcing strong boundaries in these relationships. There is no one-size-fits-all way to practice tailgate accountability. The point is to try to open your mind and heart to those who may not fit your precise belief system and to relate to them on some level—without condoning hateful ideology or putting yourself or your loved ones at risk. Even if you never agree on a single issue, your focus on building bridges, listening to understand, and finding common ground can help reduce the grievance-fueled polarization that leads people (including ourselves) to make caricatures out of someone with a different background or political persuasion. Practice this when it is safe for you to do so.

Emmett Till and the "Intimacy of Hatred" that Killed Him

Emmett Till was a fourteen-year-old Black teenager who was kidnapped and lynched in Mississippi in 1955 after he was accused of offending a white woman, Carolyn Bryant, at a grocery store. His murder was brutal, and in the aftermath his killers were tried in court and acquitted (found not guilty) by an all-white jury. The brutality of Till's murder and the acquittal of his killers epitomizes the history of violent persecution and dehumanization of Black Americans in the United States.

Professor Eddie Glaude of Princeton University reminds us that the men who murdered Till were protected by their community.[14] He explains that it is often in intimate spaces where "hatred, fear, and grievance fester" and that these places—your local hang out, card game, or, yes, tailgate—can be a space that privately normalizes hate or grievance toward people who are unlike those in the intimate group. In this case, the intimate spaces for white people in Till's Mississippi community played a role in the cover up of his murder.[15] What would have happened at the trial if one white person in the community was willing to speak out about who Till's killers were?

Using Till's murder as an example, Professor Glaude has discussed the concept of the "intimacy of hatred" and the complacency we contribute to it if we enable hatred, grievance, and fear to grow in our intimate spaces. He urges all of us to understand the responsibility we have to be accountable and to disrupt that intimacy. Part of **tailgate accountability** is calling out hatred even in spaces where people are close to us (see Step 6 above); it's not allowing the desire to "build a bridge" or a "big tent" to justify excusing people who would eradicate another person's existence or violate their human rights. We must not be the modern-day community members who protected Till's murderers. With tailgate accountability, we must call out hate when and where we see it—even if among our loved ones—and be accountable to our values. We must avoid creating places for hatred to exist in comfort. In Action 5, there are tips for how to build the type of personal courage needed to be able to call out this hatred.

REJECT THE "DIVIDE AND CONQUER" MENTALITY

As you go through the steps and practice tailgate accountability, be sure to seek genuine connection with those you engage with. You do not have to agree with your friends on all political issues; being in relationship with people with whom we disagree can make us stronger. Conflict can help us recognize a different viewpoint, and you may walk away from those conversations with a better understanding of what values or perspectives matter to another person. One of my childhood friends is a fiercely conservative law professor, and we rarely agree on political issues. Nevertheless, we hear each other, and both believe these dialogues keep us thinking with an open mind. (While conservative, this friend is deeply troubled by our current environment and the incursions on the rights of people happening under this administration. He does not support this administration's agenda. I like to think our friendship has contributed to him having a permission structure to reject a new brand of conservatism that is anti-democratic.) If we were in a place in America in which people saw one another's differences as true strengths and were comfortable with agreeing to disagree, we would be in a stronger place as a nation. As the late Congresswoman Barbara Jordan used to say, "E pluribus unum—out of many, one—it was a good idea 200 years ago and it is a good idea today."[16] Today e pluribus unum is definitely a good idea.

Who Is the MAGA Granny and What Does Her Experience Tell Us About the Harms of Polarization?

Pamela Hemphill is in her seventies. She is a former supporter of President Trump and took part in the January 6, 2021, attack on the U.S. Capitol. She livestreamed the attack on Facebook and was in the Capitol for at least twenty minutes. She was convicted and sentenced to sixty days in prison for her actions that day. In prison, she started seeing a therapist and, over the course of a few years, she came to see the movement surrounding Trump as "a cult in which you are told to believe things that do not conform to reality." When President Trump came to office for his second term, he pardoned the violent rioters and insurrectionists who had been previously prosecuted and found guilty. When he offered Hemphill a pardon, she refused it. On the fifth anniversary of January 6, 2021, Ms. Hemphill testified before Congress and said:

> I had fallen for the president's lies, just like many of his supporters. Local people had welcomed me into the circle, when I was around them. I heard them say things like "the Democrats are trying to turn this into a Communist country" or "the Radical Left wants to do away with the Constitution." The gaslighting caused a lot of fear, and I was scared. With that fear in my heart, I came here on January 6th. I went from Trump's speech to the Capitol because I thought Mr. Trump would go to the Capitol with us. I heard people saying that Trump was going to "walk down to the Capitol." So I went. Well, as you know, Donald Trump never showed, but the rioters did, and the attack began.[17]

Ms. Hemphill's account illustrates how fear and scapegoating particular groups of people (in this case, the Democrats) can take on a life of its own and lead others to engage in harmful behavior against the disparaged group. It shows how the president's tactics and those of his movement are seeking to polarize people in ways that make it impossible to come together. After being convicted and serving time, Ms. Hemphill became a supporter of the pro-democracy movement (including campaigning for Democratic candidates).

How can we create permission structures for people to accept accountability and to change their minds?

TO-DO LIST

We Hold These Truths

What Still Binds Us at 250 Years—Take the 250 Pledge

What do Lynda Carter (the American actress best known for her role as Wonder Woman), Stacey Abrams, author Jodi Picoult, and General Wesley Clark have in common? They have all signed the *We Hold These Truths* 250 Pledge. The nationwide *We Hold These Truths* initiative brings Americans of all ideologies and beliefs together behind core truths that should be uncontroversial. While we may not all agree on every issue, there are some fundamental nonnegotiable tenets that most Americans support. **Even if you are having trouble finding common ground with those who disagree with you on policy issues, you can try to seek agreement on the basic ideas underpinning our democracy.**

Within days of the initiative's launch on July 4, 2025, tens of thousands of Americans had signed up, and the support continues to grow.

NOW, TAKE ACTION

- ➔ **Read and sign.** Go to weholdtruths.org to learn more and sign the 250 Pledge.
- ➔ **Act.** Take the action steps and sign up for opportunities for action.
- ➔ **Share.** Ask your friends, loved ones, and even those who may not agree with you to read the truths and make the pledge.
- ➔ **Connect the dots.** How do these truths acknowledged by the 250 Pledge impact who you vote for? What do your elected officials believe about these principles and have they voted to back it up? Would they sign the pledge? What about

corporations, universities, and other institutions? Are they promoting these truths?

→ **Reflect.** How can you and your community support these truths as the United States embarks on the next 250 years? Share your actions.

While this chapter has been focused on understanding the forces that lead to polarization and how we can take a role in overcoming it, it is important to remember that the crisis in our nation has also resulted from millions of people opting out of our political system. Tailgate accountability can be practiced with our loved ones, with our friends, and also with those who have been taught to demonize us, those we have been taught to demonize, and those who are turned off by the mutual practice of demonization. Find your tailgate, start slowly and privately, build by identifying common group opportunities, be clear about your values and positions, share facts and admit vulnerabilities, and enforce your boundaries. Do not seek to change someone's mind, but be open to helping them shift and to shifting yourself.

ACTION 5

Get Serious About Fear, Courage, and Joy

"DAD, DOING THE RIGHT THING WILL NEVER BE THE WRONG THING." These are the words said by the teenage son of Geoff Duncan, the former Republican Lieutenant Governor in Georgia, after Donald Trump lost the election to Joe Biden and mounted a pressure campaign to throw out millions of votes in the state. As an elected Republican at the time, Geoff had taken a number of positions that I and many others oppose. Even with policy positions that many disagree with and would find indefensible, in 2020 Geoff knew it was unethical to discard ballots that had been cast, and so he took a stand against President Trump's efforts to suppress votes. Almost immediately, he received threats to his life and his family. He required around-the-clock armed security and his kids were picked on at school. Geoff did the right thing by refusing to allow the president to suppress votes, and there were costs to doing it. But, as he told members of Congress that day, it was the words from his son that gave him "the courage to stand up and keep moving."[1] (Geoff is now running for office in Georgia as a Democrat. He has expressed public regret for the prior positions he took when lieutenant governor.)

These acts of everyday courage—and the threats, harm, and retribution that have come as a result—can be seen in many walks of life, not just in the work of election officials and politicians. Take Erez Reuveni, for example, a former lawyer for the Department of Justice (DOJ) who was fired in April 2025 for refusing to lie to a federal court. Erez was a career civil servant who joined the DOJ a few years after he graduated from law school and served under Presidents Obama, Trump, Biden, and, once again, Trump. He defended the government's policies, regardless of his personal views or who was in charge, in keeping with his obligations as a civil servant and an attorney. Yet these ideals—fidelity to the U.S. Constitution and to the rule of law—put him squarely in opposition with the government when he was assigned to defend the Trump administration's removal of immigrant Abrego Garcia to El Salvador in direct contravention of a court order not to do so (see pages 15–16). The government admitted the removal was a mistake but refused to take any steps to correct that error. Instead, DOJ leadership directed Erez to argue in court that Abrego Garcia was a dangerous criminal and a terrorist, even though no evidence supporting such claims existed. When Erez refused to lie to a court about these facts, he was fired. Both Erez and his family received threats, but that didn't deter or silence him. Instead, he filed a whistleblower complaint with Congress, outlining the many ways in which the DOJ was unlawfully evading court orders and compromising professional ethics.

"I took an oath to uphold and defend the Constitution. And my view of that oath is that I need to speak up and draw attention to what has happened to the department, what is happening to the rule of law," Erez said in a *60 Minutes* interview. "I would not be faithfully abiding by my oath if I stayed silent right now."[2] (In November 2025, Erez started working as an attorney at Democracy Forward.)

Others have stayed true to their values and paid dearly for it too. By the end of 2025, more than two hundred career attorneys at the DOJ had been fired, many for doing their work instead of the government's bidding. Thousands more had resigned. Academics and educators have been terminated for expressing their views or maintaining their commitment to equity and inclusion for all. Journalists have faced pressure to change their reporting, with some losing their posts because their media outlets didn't want to bear the risk of reporting the truth and angering a thin-skinned president. Physicians have been put in positions in which they have to decide between fulfilling their oath to provide care consistent with their best medical judgment and the requirements of anti-science laws and healthcare bans passed in many states.

THE COST OF HOLDING TIGHT TO YOUR VALUES

What happened to Geoff, Erez, and countless others, is not uncommon in societies accelerating toward autocracy. Autocratic movements and leaders seek to create costs to maintaining your democratic values—or to your allegiance to anything that is not the consolidation of their power. Basics like a lawyer or doctor following their professional oath, an educator taking seriously their job to teach history and critical thinking, a reporter being committed to reporting the facts, a minister or religious leader's pledge that their house of worship serve all people, or a group of friends simply showing up to a protest can become personally and professionally risky. In general, ethical obligations, our Constitution, professional standards, and our own moral compass create guardrails that check abuses of power and allow the promise of democracy to flourish. Yet, such guardrails are not welcomed by autocratic actors, who seek to threaten people and institutions that run counter to their political agenda. Recognizing this pattern—and how it is playing out in our own nation—is the first step in responding to it.

As we take action to fight for our freedom, we must understand and get serious about fear, courage, and joy.

GETTING SERIOUS ABOUT FEAR

Anti-democracy movements and politicians use fear and the instability it brings to gain power. Fear is a common human emotion brought on by feeling physically or emotionally unsafe, by the belief that someone or something is harmful, threatening, or likely to cause us pain. It is a natural response, aimed at keeping us out of harm's way. Fear can be manipulated by those in charge to maintain and gain further power. For centuries, political philosophers have discussed how fear and chaos in the social order can lead people to seek stability, even if it is accompanied by restrictions on freedom. In 1776, John Adams wrote that "fear is the foundation of most governments," though he followed it up with "but it is so sordid and brutal a passion . . . that Americans will not be likely to approve of any political institution which is founded on it."[3]

Autocrats and anti-democratic movements capitalize on our primal human emotions and responses to tighten liberties. We have seen this happen in Putin's Russia, where the risks of speaking out against the government have increased as arrests of citizens have risen—until people decide it's safer to stay silent or self-censor and accept the new limits to their freedom.

Sometimes fear arises from external factors—like economic recession, an increase in crime, job loss due to changing industries, or external threats like a pandemic or war. In these instances, democracy-oriented political leadership seeks to use the power of government to address and mitigate fear by supporting the population and navigating the threats together. In contrast, power-hungry leaders stoke fear, using crises to hide their own incompetence, portray themselves as the only answer to the problem, and suppress opposition.

"The Only Thing We Have to Fear Is Fear Itself"

Franklin Delano Roosevelt's First Inaugural Address

As fascism raged in Europe and the Great Depression ravaged the United States, President Franklin Delano Roosevelt addressed the nation at his 1933 inauguration. Almost a century later, his words still resonate.

> This is preeminently the time to speak the truth, the whole truth, frankly and boldly. Nor need we shrink from honestly facing conditions in our country today. This great Nation will endure as it has endured, will revive and will prosper. So, first of all, let me assert my firm belief that the only thing we have to fear is fear itself—nameless, unreasoning, unjustified terror which paralyzes needed efforts to convert retreat into advance.[4]

Often, autocratic leaders instill fear through manufactured crises and intentional chaos. The Trump-Vance administration's "shock and awe" mode of government—in which a never-ending torrent of executive orders shocks the system and immigration raids in our communities and military in the streets trigger panic—has sowed fear across the nation. As part of their tactic, they have promised to root out those who are to blame, those who, in their view, stand in the way of making the country great again—Black and Brown communities, immigrants, LGBTQ people, political opponents, protesters, and activists—often relying on misinformation and disinformation campaigns.

Autocratic actors frequently seek to create a society on the brink of destruction with the understanding that they will need to take regressive steps against those deemed responsible—whether it is Viktor Orbán denigrating migrants as "poison," Marine Le Pen blaming the Muslim population and globalization for the breakdown of French society, or President Trump's rhetoric against immigrants. Research suggests that many of President Trump's early supporters were more likely than non-supporters to think the United States was on the brink of collapse.[5]

Anti-democracy actors use fear to target opponents or institutions that they perceive are not aligned with their vision. Truth-telling becomes risky and taking a stand becomes riskier still. We have seen this with the government's targeting of law firms and organizations like the American Academy of Pediatrics and the American Bar Association, as well as its attempts to cut off funds to regions of the country that Trump perceives oppose him. He has also sought to prosecute people who, as part of their jobs, investigate him or his conduct. This targeting has spread to the general public with the cooperation of platforms such as TikTok and Meta, and databases compiling the personal information of people who do not support the administration.

THE COST OF FEAR-BASED INACTION

Fearing the consequences of standing up to threats to democracy can lead to underestimating the cost of inaction. Because autocratic movements and leaders make the price of not conforming to their whims so visible, conventional wisdom suggests that it is risky not to capitulate to their demands. This can lead people and institutions to take actions that are inconsistent with their values as well as, ultimately, detrimental to their long-term well-being. People may decide not to take part in marches or protests because of the fear of arrest. Or they may rubberstamp presidential orders instead of questioning their legality out of a fear of being fired. But people and institutions in a backsliding democracy fail to realize that often the cost of capitulation is higher than the cost of standing up for your values.

Take the example of the nation's most elite law firms that were on the receiving end of the president's clearly unconstitutional executive orders because they had worked on legal actions against him. The law firms feared that if they did not capitulate to demands and settle with the White House, the president's retributive tactics would endanger their client relationships and ability to operate. Some of those firms calculated that the risk created warranted settling and they gave in to the president. Others felt the fear and risk but went to court to sue the government. In each of the cases in which the law firms took legal action and refused to cave, courts (as of the printing of this book) have ruled that the executive orders were unconstitutional and blocked them. The White House has not issued any executive orders targeting firms since then. Interestingly, some of the firms that capitulated experienced significant fallout, with protest from employees and partner resignations as well as the loss of clients who viewed them as having sold out their values in the face of fear.[6]

Sociologist Kim Lane Scheppele has studied backsliding democracies across the globe and notes that if companies choose to give up the rule of law because they believe it is good for business, "they will quickly learn they are wrong. But it will be too late."[7] While it may seem that the cost of pushing back on autocracy is high, the cost of allowing an autocratic leader or movement to consolidate power is much higher.

It's in times like these that we must look at how autocracies have played out elsewhere in the world and throughout history and learn from these examples. Autocratic leaders seek to spread fear, creating a sense of paralysis among people and movements, pushing communities underground, exhausting them, or keeping them too scared to take action altogether. In his book *They Thought They Were Free: The Germans from 1933–45*, journalist Milton Mayer explores how fear-based governing stopped people from acting until it was too late. The book was informed by interviews with ordinary Germans who lived during the Hitler years. One of the interviewees said:

> If the last and worst act of the whole regime had come immediately after the first and smallest . . . millions would have been sufficiently shocked . . . But this isn't the way it happens. In between comes all the hundreds of little steps, some imperceptible, each preparing you not to be shocked by the next . . . Suddenly it all comes down . . . You see . . . what you have done, or, more accurately, what you haven't done (for that was all that was required of most of us: that we do nothing). You remember those early meetings of your department in the university when, if one had stood, others would have stood, but no one stood. You remember everything now, and your heart breaks. Too late.[8]

Every day I speak with people who are scared by what is going on in this country, who are terrified by what may happen next. I acknowledge and validate their fear. I also gently ask them to accept that things have escalated rapidly over the course of the last few months and that things will likely get worse. We have to look fear in the face and act now—while we still can. For that, we'll need to embrace courage.

Understanding courage. Courage is rarely a knight in shining armor, charging confidently into battle. Courage cannot, in fact, exist without fear: *It is a decision we can make in response to fear.* It must arise in a person who is quaking in their boots, choosing to prioritize their values and integrity and act in spite of what they feel, even when there is a cost. Courage comes from the Latin word *cor,* or heart. It can mean to speak your truth or your heart—to do what you know is right and good.

The courage of ordinary people is essential for our democracy, yet we must learn to build our practice of courage. It requires vulnerability, risk, and being uncomfortable. And this requires hard work—we must offer ourselves grace as we learn.

In 1910 in Paris, President Teddy Roosevelt gave a speech that emphasized that living in a nation that aspires to be a great republic calls for all citizens to be responsible. An often-quoted passage, known as "Man in the Arena," has captured the minds of many in contemporary times, informing leadership trainings for CEOs and providing a road map for how people can live more authentically. The passage from Roosevelt reads:

> It is not the critic who counts; not the man who points out how the strong man stumbles, or where the doer of deeds could have done them better. The credit belongs to the man who is actually ***in the arena*** [emphasis added], whose face is marred by dust and sweat and blood; who strives valiantly;

> who errs and comes short again and again, because there is no effort without error or shortcoming; but who does actually strive to do the deeds; who knows the great enthusiasms, the great devotions; who spends himself in a worthy cause; who at the best knows in the end the triumph of high achievement, and who, at the worst, if he fails, at least fails while daring greatly, so that his place shall never be with those cold and timid souls who neither know victory nor defeat.[9]

These words were intended to inspire ordinary people, who lived in what Roosevelt calls "the great republics," to find courage and lean into the work of our democracy.

Indeed, democracy requires constant vigilance. It requires that people use the tools they have—their community connections and vocations; their access to litigation; and their rights to protest, vote, speak freely, and assemble—to mount challenges when rights are violated or when people are not served by their government. The grave threats to individual freedom that the United States have faced in the past—from the scourge of Jim Crow to the prosecution of political dissidents prior to World War I to the two Red Scares and more—required a courageous response from people who were unwilling to bow down to fear. People who refused to go along to get along and followed their values—their hearts—even when there was a cost. Imagine what the aftermath of the 2020 election would have looked like had Geoff Duncan, or countless other election workers across the country, given into intimidation tactics.

"Democracy Requires Your Courage"

In February 2025, Illinois Governor JB Pritzker, who knew that his state would be targeted by the Trump-Vance administration, addressed rising threats to diversity, equity, and inclusion initiatives in his State of the State speech to the Illinois Legislature. He reminded us all:

> Tyranny requires your fear and your silence and your compliance. Democracy requires your courage. So gather your justice and humanity . . . and do not let the "tragic spirit of despair" overcome us when our country needs us the most.[10]

Courage is the new currency. In this moment in American life, we need courage. It is the way we will get from where we are to where we need to go—from a democracy backsliding into autocracy to one that is reimagined and serves all people. This is not the first time we have seen tyranny in the United States. The nation was founded as an experiment in a government that professed to be of, by, and for the people—a government that rejected a king. Yet this is a nation that was built on the backs of human enslavement, dehumanization, and land theft—where freedom was only for some, not for all. The history of the journey for democracy in this nation is one of fighting tyrannies of many kinds. The singular commonality has been the role of courage. What's old is new again. Courage is the new currency.

Harriet Tubman is the embodiment of courage. She was born into slavery in 1822 in Maryland and at twenty-seven, she escaped and reached Philadelphia, Pennsylvania. There she worked with abolitionists, but that wasn't all. Despite the risk, she returned to the South many times, knowing that there was a bounty on her head, making thirteen trips over ten years. She guided more than seventy people north to freedom, and she led a military operation that destroyed Confederate supplies and helped hundreds of enslaved people escape. In 2022, the U.S. Central Intelligence Agency installed a statue of Tubman on its grounds, celebrating her as a model spy and champion of courage.[11]

After Frederick Douglass escaped from slavery to become a free man in New York, he chose to build a movement for abolition and to take on the powerful. He could have made a long list of reasons why it was risky for him to confront political leaders publicly and found more comfortable ways to resist. Yet he chose courage at every turn. He reminds us:

> This struggle may be a moral one, or it may be a physical one, and it may be both moral and physical, but it must be a struggle. Power concedes nothing without a demand. It never did and it never will.[12]

This sentiment was echoed more than a century later by Dr. Martin Luther King Jr., who moved back to the South, away from the relative comfort of his circles in Boston, to advance the civil rights movement. He was arrested twenty-nine times at the hands of state and local governments who defended segregation.[13] While in the Birmingham City Jail in Alabama, he wrote a letter to white moderate clergy members who knew of the horror of segregation and Jim Crow but chose to wait on the sidelines and criticized King's nonviolent, direct action as too aggressive. In his *Letter from Birmingham Jail,* he expressed disappointment that they had chosen to be "more cautious than courageous and have remained silent behind the anesthetizing security" of the status quo.[14]

TIP SHEET

Resources for People of Faith and Moral Commitments

Approximately 74 percent of people in the U.S. identify as people of faith. Throughout U.S. history, faith communities and people with secular moral commitments have played a key role in showing courage in the face of injustice. At the same time, religious extremism threatens our rights, democracy, and communities. Perversely, religious extremists (who do not represent the vast majority of people of faith) often claim they are the only "true believers" and seek to monopolize religious faith against values like equality, inclusion, and civil rights. Don't let them claim your faith.

Consider learning more about the Interfaith Alliance (interfaithalliance.org), an organization that offers opportunities for people of diverse faiths and beliefs to take action. Your faith can be a critical force for good in this moment. For more information on ways to be part of the pro-democracy faith movement, visit ordinarypeopleaction.com.

Complacency has always been a threat to achieving the promise of our democracy, yet it has increased since the end of the Cold War and amid the hopeful progress of the civil rights era. Ordinary people and many in power seem to have convinced themselves that freedom is a given, that the comfort of their day-to-day lives is more important than the continued work for progress. Too many instances of police brutality and the killing of Black men at the hands of law enforcement and armed citizens took place before people reacted with outrage and national protests in the aftermath of Breonna Taylor's and George Floyd's murders. Likewise, the vast majority of people in this country oppose bans on reproductive healthcare, including abortion, but those rights were curtailed by multiple states for decades without much pushback. It was only after the Court's decision to reverse *Roe v. Wade* in 2022 that a significant outcry took place.[15]

Since Trump's second inauguration, ordinary people in this nation have understood that the threat to democratic freedoms for all is real. People are protesting in historic numbers and many who do not consider themselves civically active are getting involved. We must all find the courage to take action consistent with our values when we are called upon—whether at the ballot box or in a corporate board room, government job, or school board meeting; when unaccountable federal agents descend on our streets; or in our families and communities, faith circles, and other settings—or we risk losing it all.

As part of taking action, we must all get serious about courage—and practice it each day in small ways, so that—together—we make a big impact. Here are some steps to help.

TAKE EIGHT STEPS TO BUILD COURAGE

Step 1. Define and clarify your values. Ground yourself in your values and in the values you wish to see in our nation. Reflect on them. Some people find it useful to write them down—or even write a mission statement. Remember the story of Geoff Duncan. He and his family had a family motto, "Doing the right thing will never be the wrong thing." In the context of national politics, one value could be "country over party." Some of you may have religious commitments, such as "love thy neighbor," that form the basis of your personal values.

Step 2. Courage is a practice. Fake it until you make it. Courage may not come to us easily, and it is important to find small ways to try it out—to build the muscle of prioritizing your values over your comfort. You might speak up in a small group about your beliefs or on behalf of a colleague or neighbor. You could attend peaceful protests, even if they make you uneasy. If you are in a professional situation where there is pressure to compromise your ethics, refuse to do so (or make a plan with your loved ones about what you will do if the time comes). If your workplace has pulled back on its commitment to diversity, equality, and inclusion, you might think of small steps to resist. If you live in a community that "others" people in harmful ways, show visible support for the people targeted. Social research suggests that the presence of even a single dissenting voice can help others find their own voice, clarify their values, and not capitulate to dominant views.[16] You may have beliefs, allegiances, or practices that you question—changing your perspective is also a courageous action. Find places and ways you can practice courage.

Step 3. Examine where your courage is needed and make a plan. Think about your specific circumstances and where your courage or your voice is needed—and then be intentional about showing up with courage every day.

Step 4. Courage is contagious. Build community so you don't have to always go it alone. We've seen that autocrats aim to isolate and make us forget our common humanity. When loneliness sets in, it can lead people to be less courageous or motivated by their values. On the flip side, when people are in community and join together to take action, courage is contagious. Be intentional about creating spaces where you do not feel alone. On the To-Do List at the end of this chapter you will find resources for how to gather people together to help build courage as part of Dinners for Democracy.

Step 5. Ground your actions in gratitude for our courageous friends and ancestors. We know that many who came before us exhibited great courage. Reflecting on them and their actions can help ground us and our actions now. Some of you may have family members or friends who have shown personal courage. Others may be inspired by historical figures. Learning about more people who have demonstrated courage can be a key way to build gratitude and motivate us to take steps toward courage.

Think about the present too. If you know someone, an organization, or a business that has exhibited courage, write and thank them. If you are an alum of a university that stands up to abuses of power, tell them you appreciate it. If you are a fan of a musician or sports team that exhibits principle, let your gratitude be known. If you see a community member being courageous, tell them you see it. It matters to people to know that their actions are noticed.

Step 6. Approach fear with curiosity. Ask questions about why you are fearful so that you can understand your underlying feelings. Are there ways to mitigate the costs you are worried about? Think about discussing your fears with a trusted person in your life so that you can walk through them together.

Step 7. Do not let the cost of acting lead you to underestimate the cost of inaction. If you weigh the risks and benefits of action, be sure to weigh the cost of inaction. What happens if you don't lean into your values? What happens if no one checks the abuse of power? The cost of inaction is often far greater than the cost of action.

Step 8. Just Do It. You know in your heart what the right thing is to do. Courage is a word of the heart—it is your personal truth. So, in the end, take the leap. It is okay to be afraid. It is okay to start small. Or to make a mistake. Being courageous also means having the vulnerability to try new things, to fail, and try again. As Teddy Roosevelt reminds us—don't let the (inner) critic count! But make the choice to act in the face of fear. You will be glad you did.

TO-DO LIST

Read or watch a movie about a person who has exhibited courage or someone who inspires you. This is a great step for young people too. Suggestions are on ordinarypeopleaction.com.

NEXT, EMBRACE JOY

Our work and outlook in this moment does not have to be all grim. It may seem counterintuitive to be joyful while people are being shot in our streets and the very government that is supposed to protect us instead harms us. But humans across the world and across time have found ways to experience joy even in the darkest circumstances—joy has fueled movements for justice and freedom. Indeed, it sustains us on a long and difficult journey. We must challenge ourselves to find joy.

Joy is important to the work of opposing extremism, fighting for freedom, and reimagining democracies. In terror-inducing circumstances, finding joy is an act of resistance. Just as building community is a statement of defiance against autocratic forces that seek to divide us, embracing joy stands in opposition to the fear that autocratic actors aim to impose.

Finding and embracing joy is also a way to lay the foundations for the world that we want to create in the future. The poet Jack Gilbert in his "A Brief for the Defense" summarizes the role of joy in times of joylessness:

> If we deny our happiness, resist our satisfaction,
> we lessen the importance of their deprivation.[17]

If we are not able to experience joy when it is available, we cheapen what we are fighting for. Joy enables us to replenish our emotional reserves so we can take action and contribute in this moment. It is a condition that brings us into ourselves—it reminds us how to stay human, to soften our hearts, when outside forces or the misery of the world would seek to harden us. It is a way of embracing our rituals and culture—and remembering what we are fighting for.

The Jewish German political theorist and philosopher Hannah Arendt, renowned for her writing on totalitarianism and "the banality of evil," knew firsthand the terrors of living under the Nazi regime. During World War II, she was arrested and detained by the French government as an "enemy alien" and sent to a French concentration camp. She wrote in 1955:

> I've begun so late, really only in recent years, to truly love the world . . . Out of gratitude, I want to call my book on political theories *Amor Mundi*.[18]

Arendt did not have a sanguine attitude about humanity or the world—she was well aware of the cruelty and violence that existed—yet she found a way to soften her heart with gratitude and love.

Joy is a love for the world we want to create—and a belief that we can create it—that we must be sure to find, even in difficult times. This can sustain us personally as well as fuel our work to bring about a better reality.

There Will Be Dancing and Art at the Revolution

Throughout history and in the present, people targeted by their government or in other dehumanizing circumstances have turned to music, art, dancing, theatre, literature, and other creative expression to find joy and affirm their inherent dignity and the dignity of their communities. In April 1992, the siege of Sarajevo began when Serbian nationalist forces blockaded the capital in what would be *the* longest siege of a capital city in history (three times longer than the Battle of Stalingrad in World War II).[19] People were terrorized and bombing was nearly constant, stretching over 1,425 days of siege. Sarajevans sustained long periods without water, electricity, and basic necessities. Amid the bombs, fear, terror, and destruction, art became resistance: The Sarajevo Philharmonic Orchestra continued to perform sixty unique concerts, the Sarajevo String Quartet played over two hundred shows, and over two thousand theatrical performances were put on.[20]

"Either we cried, or we kept working," Miodrag Trifunov, one of the founders of the Sarajevo War Theatre, stated. "We chose the latter."[21]

Of course, Sarajevo is just one example of the resilience of ordinary people who find themselves in extraordinary times holding to their humanity through finding joy and beauty. There are countless accounts from our own nation's history as well as from the present. Many enslaved people in the Antebellum South found ways through music and ritual to defy the culture of their oppressors. Defying oppressors and turning to joy was a key strategy of the twentieth-century civil rights, women's rights, worker's rights, and anti-war movements. Do you remember or have you heard about Woodstock? A profoundly political musical festival, Woodstock questioned and opposed the Vietnam War and pushed for greater rights for people.

Dubbed "Three Days of Peace and Music," the festival brought about solidarity, community, and hope as so many Americans were drafted into and died in a war that many opposed. In the fight for LGBTQ rights following police raids targeting the queer community at Stonewall, members of the LGBTQ community and their allies danced in an act of defiance and resistance of systemic oppression.[22] Joy and beauty are acts of resistance and are ways of holding on to our inherent dignity and freedom as individuals. Learn more at ordinarypeopleaction.com about the history of joy and beauty as a form of resistance—and how we can leverage that rich history in our present time.

TIP SHEET

Pathways to Joy

Finding joy in a bleak time is different for each person. Here are some tips to get you started. You'll find more options, including an invitation to share how you're finding joy, at ordinarypeopleaction.com.

- ➔ **Practice habits of daily joy.** Identify what you can do every day that brings you joy. It could be taking a walk, listening to music, reading a book or poetry, calling a friend, playing with a pet or your kids. Be intentional about your daily habits, and focus on the joy you get from them, even if momentary.
- ➔ **Focus on rituals.** Try to keep rituals—meaningful habits that bring you joy—alive, or create new ones. Do you like to watch sports on the weekend or listen to live music? Perhaps you prefer to meditate, sit quietly, or bake bread. Or attend a religious

service. Find something that you like and build a ritual around it at least a few times a year.

- **Embrace gratitude.** Gratitude is one of the largest contributors to joy. Focus on what you are grateful for—perhaps your health, relationships, food and shelter, the capacity to learn, and to be in community. A gratitude journal can help contribute to joy.
- **Don't forget art and nature.** Your ability to experience the beauty in art or nature may vary depending on where you live and your circumstances. But focus on how you can try to access art and nature each day—it could be a favorite song or part of a film. I enjoy poetry and find it easy to process in bits. Watching the sun set or going outside at night to gaze at the vast sky or stars can be a way of capturing joy. Some find comfort and joy in creating art or working in nature by planting gardens, tending to a yard or patio plants, or setting up a bird feeder.
- **Laugh out loud.** Laughing and humor are important contributors to joy, and they have long fueled social movements. When was the last time you laughed—really laughed? If you've gone a few days without doing so, think about how you might change that. Chatting with a funny friend, watching an amusing video, or playing with a pet can inspire laughter.
- **Strengthen community.** As with building courage, community is also important to joy. Find ways to engage with people to enhance your connection. This can lead to opportunities to find joy with one another.

Poet Jane Hirshfield's beautiful poem "The Weighing" celebrates the restorative nature of joy. It can give us the strength to carry on in this difficult time. She ends with the lines:

> So few grains of happiness
> measured against all the dark
> and still the scales balance.
> The world asks of us
> only the strength we have and we give it.
> Then it asks more, and we give it.[23]

TO-DO LIST

Community Creates Conditions for Courage & Finding Joy

Host a Dinner for Democracy or Coffee for Change

As our team at Democracy Forward has heard from people across the nation who felt alone and were searching for ways to cope, we began Dinners for Democracy and Coffee for Change to encourage people to connect with one another.

Within months, Americans in all fifty states had started hosting dinners or coffees in their homes, yards, and neighborhoods—or virtually. From retirement communities to high school hangouts, people are gathering and engaging. Community became a foundation for finding courage and embracing joy. Take action by visiting democracyforward.org/dinners to learn more.

ACTION 6

Remember the Past, Fight for the Future

"WE'VE SEEN THIS OVER AND OVER AGAIN," a well-known cable news anchor said briskly to me on live television. Our team at Democracy Forward had just won a court order to stop President Trump from discontinuing the federal Supplemental Nutrition Assistance Program (SNAP) during the government shutdown—risking food loss to more than forty million people. "You win in the lower court, and then the Supreme Court without explanation blocks your win. Will this court order really help people?"[1] I responded quickly that the order *would* enable people to get their nutritional assistance (it did) and that we didn't believe the Supreme Court would have a basis for blocking it.

While I was confident in my answers, the question that the news anchor was asking—*What do we do about the Supreme Court?*—is on the minds of many. In our system of government, the courts are supposed to check governmental power when the rights of people are violated—whether that power is exercised by a local government, a state, Congress, or the president and federal agencies within the executive branch. While there are hundreds of courts across the nation that provide this check, the Supreme Court—which holds the final word on the interpretation of the Constitution—has a particular responsibility to ensure that the American people's rights are protected, including from their government. Many Americans believe it has not done so.

The approval rating of the Supreme Court is at historic lows. When courts fail to perform their checks and balances function or to be perceived as impartially administrating justice, they face a legitimacy crisis. That's where the Supreme Court is today, and people are rightly concerned, but, as we will see, this isn't the first time in its history that the Court has faced this crisis. Part of doing the work to protect our rights and the rights of our neighbors involves understanding the role of courts, including the U.S. Supreme Court—but it also involves understanding our history and how ordinary people have created real change even against long odds. Both our present and our history show that the courts can be simultaneously one of the greatest tools and the biggest hurdles in the protection of the rights of the people of this country.

In this chapter, we take a look at the courts in our current time (plus how we can use them to protect our rights and take action to ensure our courts do justice). We also explore how our history can inform the actions we take today. The past reminds us that the courts, along with many institutions in our democracy, were not built to hold all of us. Women, people of color, white men who were not property owners, immigrants, LGBTQ people—we were all left out of the founders' plans 250 years ago.

History teaches us that our generation's work is similar to the work of prior generations: to bring about a future where we all are represented and achieve a democracy that holds all of us. There are tools ordinary people have used throughout history to make systematic change that we need to use today. Knowledge of our past will help lead us toward the future we must create. Not a future that is simply a restoration of the old days, but one that brings about true democracy for all. Ordinary people will drive that change, and we must take action to do it.

THE COURT IN CRISIS

For a democratic republic to truly protect the rights of people, courts must act when individual rights are violated by the government. (Autocratic regimes, such as in Iran and China, significantly limit the ability of citizens to take meaningful action in courts to challenge their governments for individual rights abuses.) Our Constitution is largely enforced through the courts—and the U.S. Supreme Court has the final say on the interpretation of our United States Constitution. Our democratic system therefore depends on the people's faith in the courts and the rule of law. The adage *We are a nation of laws, not men* does not hold if courts do not act to ensure that the law protects people from the arbitrary whims of a ruler.

The American people understand this. The courts remain the most trusted of the three branches of government, even as trust in institutions of all sorts have been dropping. Yet, in recent years, the people's trust in the U.S. Supreme Court has taken a nosedive, foreshadowing the larger wave of declining confidence in our democratic institutions. In 2024, just 35 percent of people in the nation had confidence in the U.S. Supreme Court.[2]

The United States Supreme Court's most recent legitimacy crisis has been building for some time but intensified when President Obama nominated a replacement to the Court after Justice Antonin Scalia's death in February 2016. The nomination was met with a campaign, "Let the People Decide," funded by the far-right Judicial Crisis Network (JCN), which pressured the U.S. Senate to re-

Not Just One Court . . .

While confidence in the U.S. Supreme Court is at historic lows, people still have a relatively high amount of confidence in their state and local courts. Later in this chapter, we explore how you can take action to support fair courts, including at the state and local levels. To learn more about how our court system is structured, go to ordinarypeopleaction.com.

fuse to vote, insisting that whoever won the upcoming presidential election should appoint the next justice.[3] This special interest pressure campaign worked, and the Senate never presented President Obama's nominee (then federal circuit judge Merrick Garland) for a vote. When President Trump assumed office in January 2017, he appointed his nominee, and the Senate quickly confirmed Neil Gorsuch to replace Justice Scalia. Then, after pressure from outside groups, U.S. Supreme Court Associate Justice Anthony Kennedy retired from the Court, enabling President Trump to appoint a second justice (Brett Kavanaugh), shifting the Court further.

Toward the end of the first Trump administration—just under two months before the 2020 election—Justice Ruth Bader Ginsburg died. The special interest groups that had insisted on waiting to fill the vacancy on the Court left by Justice Scalia eight months before the 2016 election quickly changed their tune. They pressured the Senate to rush through the confirmation of Justice Amy Coney Barrett *just weeks before* the 2020 election and the Senate did so. This resulted in the Court that we have today. For many, this packing of the Court by President Trump (with the assistance of outside groups such as JCN and The Federalist Society, which selected and vetted judicial candidates) has caused grave concerns for the Court's legitimacy.

Other factors have also played a role in the Court's current legitimacy crisis. The Court reversed or weakened decisions on critical rights for people, including the right to privacy as it relates to abortion, ending five decades of constitutional federal protection under *Roe v. Wade*. The opinion in *Dobbs v. Jackson Women's Health Organization* (the decision that reversed *Roe*) was leaked weeks before the Court issued its ruling, disrupting the Court's norms and raising concerns about politization.[4] The majority decision, written by Justice Alito, contained language used by far-right activist organizations, such as Faith in Action, that had worked to unofficially sway Supreme Court justices (through "prayer sessions") to gain support for anti-choice positions.[5] This raised questions regarding influences on the Court, especially the influences of religious special interest groups. The Court's decision in *Dobbs* caused public outcry. Then, a year later, there was more cause for concern. The majority's decision in *Trump v. United States* found the president had absolute immunity under federal law for actions taken in his official capacity. This decision has been widely viewed as providing the president with king-like power and undermining the people's ability to hold the president accountable. As this book is going to print, the Court has eviscerated Section 2 of the Voting Rights Act, which is ushering in even more subversion of representation of Black and Brown communities in the South.

Concerns regarding outside influences (like in *Dobbs*) and conflicts of interest, especially among the Court's right wing, have raised questions about ethics. Reports that Justice Clarence Thomas accepted and failed to disclose luxury gifts on multiple occasions have caused people to question the integrity of the Court and brought to light the lack of an enforceable ethics code as it applies to the Supreme Court.

And then there's the Court's emergency docket, known as its

"shadow docket," which is what the TV anchor had been asking about after our SNAP win. When the Court decides matters on its shadow docket (as opposed to its merits docket) it generally makes decisions on an incomplete record, without argument or full briefing. Its orders are rarely explained to the public, nor do they include opinions or reasoning, which further strains the Court's legitimacy in the eyes of the American public. It's intended for true emergencies in which the Court must act quickly to preserve the status quo (for example, to pause an execution or halt a deportation), but the Trump administration has used the emergency docket with unparalleled frequency, asking the Court to stay or pause lower court orders that have ruled against the government.

Far from preserving the status quo, most of these decisions have enabled the president to disrupt it, casting aside lower court orders that were put in place to try to prevent harm until the court can fully consider the legality of the government's actions. The Trump administration has asked—and the Supreme Court has agreed—to intervene using the shadow docket exponentially more times than any presidential administration in the past. Many of the shadow docket cases the Court has decided on raise significant questions of legal interpretation, yet the Court is making decisions without full public briefing, arguments, and merits consideration. Often, the decisions are publicized in a summary of one or two lines, depriving the American people of the means of understanding the Court's reasoning behind its rulings.

Frequent use of the shadow docket has been criticized by Justices Elena Kagan, Sonia Sotomayor, and Ketanji Brown Jackson as well as legal scholars. "Our emergency docket, while fit for some times, should not be used to overrule existing law," Justice Kagan wrote in a dissent joined by Justices Sotomayor and Jackson.[6] Legal scholar and University of California Berkeley Law School

Dean Erwin Chemerinsky wrote recently with regard to the shadow docket, "'Because I said so' never is persuasive or satisfying. And it certainly should not be regarded as acceptable when it is the Supreme Court resolving important issues—even matters of life and death—without the slightest explanation."[7]

In the past year alone, the Court has undermined the Voting Rights Act, blocked lower court orders that would have protected the federal workforce, stopped the decimation of the Department of Education, and protected people's private and personal information from the Elon Musk–led DOGE. These types of decisions, which denote a marked departure from the prior practice of the Court, have left Americans worried about whether the Supreme Court will protect their rights and serve as an essential check on the administration. Indeed, the U.S. Supreme Court's failure to consistently protect the individual rights of people—from voting rights to privacy rights—is one of the causes researchers give for the United States' democratic backslide, and this failure existed prior to the current Trump administration.

COURTS AS A GUARDRAIL AGAINST AUTOCRACY

Of course, the president has not prevailed at the U.S. Supreme Court in all cases. The Court blocked the president's tariffs policy, refused to block lower court orders that ruled the president's deployment of the National Guard in Illinois was unlawful, and did not allow the administration to rush to invalidate California voters' approval of new maps. Lawyers, including me and my colleagues at Democracy Forward, who are challenging the administration in the courts believe we will prevail at the Supreme Court in a number of cases. Yet, it is shortsighted to ignore the harms of the Court's shadow docket and the crisis of confidence the public has in the

Court. It is naïve for people to believe the courts alone are going to fully protect them.

Yet our courts can buy us time for the people's voices to be heard—and that is what they have been doing. Courts across the country—lower federal courts and state courts—have provided strong guardrails against the Trump-Vance administration's incursions on the peoples' everyday rights. Indeed, many people (including those in elite circles) who have viewed taking action through the courts as hopeless in the past, have found that they underestimated the power of the courts to protect people and our democracy. As of this writing, there have been hundreds (approaching one thousand) cases filed to protect people's rights against the federal government's abuses of power, and judges of all ideological backgrounds—including those appointed by President Trump himself—have ruled against the president's unlawful actions.

Our team at Democracy Forward has secured court orders that include protecting people's right to access a lawyer, their rights to essential services, to express themselves freely, to due process, and so much more. In the context of the Trump-Vance administration, the administration is losing in court far more than it is winning. Still, very few of the cases filed against the administration have gone or are expected to go to the U.S. Supreme Court, even when considering the Trump administration's unprecedented use of the shadow docket.[8] And, as noted, the administration will not always prevail at the Supreme Court as we have seen (as of the date this book is going to print) in the context of tariffs, redistricting, and national guard deployments. In addition, the administration has backed off or abandoned its policies and agendas in the face of public pressure that arises from people making their voices heard in court. The president and his administration know that the legal pushback in the courts is working to slow their harmful agenda, leading the president to threaten judges and lawyers. **Yet, even with these successes, it is the people—not the courts—who will ultimately do the work of stopping our democratic backslide and rebuilding democracy.** This is true now—and it has been true throughout our nation's history. Remembering the past together can help us take action to reimagine our future.

REMEMBERING OUR PAST

For those who worry about the U.S. Supreme Court, it is important to remember that this is not the first time in history the Court has left people and communities disappointed. We must not gloss over the injustices that have been prevalent throughout the history of our country, nor must we confuse ourselves in thinking that any institution—be it the courts, corporations, universities, or the federal government alone—will save us. History teaches us that it is the people who will hold the responsibility of carrying our nation from where it is today to a better future, not a court that "hands down" justice or a president who signs a law. Instead, major changes only happen when the people demand that our institutions serve us—all of us.

Indeed, when we think about the Supreme Court and its role in delivering justice, many of us think about a few decades in the twentieth century, from the mid-1950s to the early '70s, and a smattering of instances earlier this century when the Court helped advance constitutional protections and rights for all. Decisions like *Brown v. Board of Education* (1954), which required that public education be available on an equal basis; *Miranda v. Arizona* (1966), which required people held in police custody be informed of their constitutional rights; *Griswold v. Connecticut* (1965), which extended the right to privacy to include contraception; *Roe v. Wade* (1973), which granted the right to privacy to termination of pregnancy through abortion; and *Loving v. Virginia* (1967), which struck down laws that prohibited interracial marriage—all arose from cases in which the Court recognized an expansion of rights for people who had been left out or subjugated by our nation's earlier systems. These cases all occurred over the course of a little more than two decades and represented real progress for people and communities—but this era when the U.S. Supreme Court consistently recognized greater freedoms and rights for people was short lived. It was the exception in U.S. legal history, not the rule.

Since the Court's decision in *Brown v. Board,* far right and conservative interests have worked to fuel a massive backlash to reverse privacy, civil rights, and civil liberties protections, stoking fear and inciting "culture wars" against LGBTQ rights, abortion rights, and DEI initiatives to build political power. Corporate interests found common cause with this effort and engaged in their own multi-decade campaign to shape the law and the courts to be friendlier to their own business interests. Such interests still view social reform legislation and other policy that seeks to regulate large enterprises with skepticism. The Court's 2015 decision in *Obergefell v. Hodges,* affirming that the right to marry is not confined to opposite sex couples, is one of the few expansions of recognized rights in the twenty-first century.

DEMOCRACY RESTRICTED

The failures of the Supreme Court historically to recognize the rights of all and to consistently check abuses of governmental power dates back to the creation of the Court itself, following the ratification of the Constitution. The Supreme Court, like all of our longstanding institutions, was not initially crafted with a democracy in which everyone is represented in mind. At the time of its inception, most states restricted voting to white male landowners; roughly 6 percent of the population. Our country's systems and structures—from the Declaration of Independence to the Constitution to laws that created the Supreme Court and other institutions—were not intended to hold all of us. Since they were first written into the Declaration of Independence, our ideals have been tested and the promises of our nation have rung hollow for many.

Thus, the Court's decisions over the past centuries often reflected a restricted democracy. Well-known decisions like *Dred Scott v. Sanford* in the 1800s (protecting the institution of slavery) and *Plessy v. Ferguson* (finding that racial segregation in schools was justified under the "separate but equal" doctrine) demonstrate the Supreme Court's failure to deliver justice or check the government's power in the advancement of people's freedom. Lesser-known examples include *Bradwell v. Illinois* (1873), in which the Court found that women do not have a right to become active members of the legal profession because, in the words of one justice, they are ordained by God to be wives and mothers—a ruling that is incompatible with holding positions in civic life.

There are examples from the twentieth century such as *Buck v. Bell* (that affirmed a law that required sterilization of people living with mental disabilities) and *Korematsu v. United States* (that upheld the justification of the United States's forced incarceration of Japanese Americans on the basis of their ethnicity during World War II). During and after the Great Depression, the Supreme Court was an impediment to social reform legislation, including cases to protect workers' rights. This caused President Franklin Delano Roosevelt to propose to "pack the court," or expand the number of justices on the Court, to reform it.

The worry that so many people have about our Supreme Court today is understandable—but it is not new. And it is certainly not a reason to descend into apathetic spectatorship or to give up. Progress in this country has been driven by the people; our institutions haven't moved on their own. The late Congresswoman Barbara Jordan, in her opening remarks before the House Judiciary Committee during the Watergate hearings of the 1970s, explained what our history means for the vast majority of us who were left out of the creation of our systems and structures in the beginning:

> "We, the people." It's a very eloquent beginning. But when that document was completed on the seventeenth of September in 1787, I was not included in that "We, the people." I felt somehow for many years that George Washington and Alexander Hamilton just left me out by mistake. But through the process of amendment, interpretation, and court decision, I have finally been included in "We, the people."[9]

Jordan then explained that her "faith in the Constitution" was "whole," "complete," and "total."[10] She said this not because of her faith in institutions but because of her faith in the role that "we, the people" play in our democracy. We, the people, can bring about a democracy that one can have faith in.

The journey of American democracy has been one of the people demanding that words become actions—and that the promises made for *all*—really include *all of us.* The situation is dire in our present moment. But the fight for democracy is not a new one. Systems of power—whether the president, the Supreme Court, other governmental power structures, or corporate power—are not set up to give in to the people's demands quickly or lightly. And so, in this moment, we must remember the past as we fight for the future.

This action step extends far beyond the courts and is important for contending with rising corporate power, autocratic movements, and our current president and Congress. Throughout history, ordinary people can, and have, made a difference through collectively demanding better. We must do that now.

FIGHT FOR THE FUTURE

So what does that future look like? I cannot tell you how many meetings I have been in over the past year in which elite academics, philanthropists, former government officials, and other leaders have wanted to talk about how we will rebuild democracy. Ordinary people I speak with across the nation also want to talk about what will happen on the other side of our current crisis. But I have noted a difference between what I've heard from the powerful and what I have heard from the people.

Those in power are interested in restoring what we used to have and their position in it, whereas the people are far more interested in reimagining what can be built in its place. The people—that is, ordinary people—know our democracy, for all its positives, has not been delivering for the majority of us for a long time. As mentioned above, this was true long before Donald Trump's arrival on the political scene.

THE IMPERATIVE OF BOLD CHANGE: REIMAGINING AS A FORM OF REBUILDING

The question is what do we want as we rebuild—to restore the old systems or reimagine them and build new systems that serve *all of us*?

The people's answer is clear: We want to reimagine our society and democracy so that it serves all of us. History's answer is clear too: The systems and structures in our democracy were not built to hold all of us, and as we build the future, we have an opportunity to create a democracy that does consider and serve all. *We must rebuild democracy through reimagining it.*

And this is where the people—that's you—come in. As we strive to defend our rights and counter a vastly accelerating autocracy, we must, at the same time, pursue bold ideas and big change—and this requires that all of us take small steps that, when taken together, can change the world and realize a new future.

What does that mean in practice? It means that we must say no to small thinking and the belief that our nation does not have the capacity for transformation—we must demand that our government and those who serve us make big changes. We must demand that those in elected governmental positions actually *use their power* to deliver for all of us—and we must build our people power to make sure those demands are met with action.

This starts with understanding the problems we need to solve and the big dreams we need to make our reality—addressing everything from affordability and accountability to opportunity. We should not be satisfied with a government that provides tax breaks and even subsidies for billionaires but cannot deliver a system in which working people are able to make ends meet, let alone flourish. Nor should we let technology oligarchs run our social contract by replacing the backbone of the American economy—its workforce—with unregulated artificial intelligence and environmentally damaging data centers. Technology is—and has always been—key to the future, but ensuring technology serves humanity and our common good is the role of government. We should demand this. We should not settle for an education system that puts learning out of reach for so many or an election system that makes it hard for people to vote and be represented fairly. And we should not settle for a government that doesn't seek to be a leader in the global effort to address climate change and environmental degradation.

And, no, we should not be satisfied with a system of justice in which the nation's highest court operates in the shadows and issues unprecedented numbers of orders affecting their interpretation of federal law and our personal freedoms without explanation, full briefing, or argument. "No right is safe in the new legal regime," Justice Sotomayor, in her dissent, warns the American people,[11] referring to the Court's excessive use of the shadow docket and seemingly automatic tendency to trample on lower court orders that protect the rights of people by refusing to hear arguments, consider full briefings, or explain its decisions.

There are no kings in the United States—and that goes for all branches of government. No kings in the White House but also no kings in black robes in courthouses. The Constitution permits Congress to pass reforms on the way the Supreme Court operates, to insist on an enforceable code of ethics, and to take other steps that could ensure accountability. Our government has the tools to insist on an ethical court. We must use our power as people to demand that the courts, and especially the Supreme Court, reflect, represent, and protect the American people and our Constitution. We must push for ethical and systematic reforms as well as for the nomination and confirmation of judges who will uphold the Constitution. This involves insisting that Congress fulfill its role, that future presidents do their jobs, and that we use our voice when the Court engages in unethical or unjust conduct.

TIP SHEET

How to Support Fair Courts

For those motivated to support fair courts, here are some options for action (further information and resources can be found at ordinarypeopleaction.com):

IF YOU HAVE LESS THAN A DAY

→ **Make sure your U.S. senators know that you care about federal judges.** Look up your U.S. senators' records on judicial confirmations and judges. You can do this online through your senators' websites or visit ordinarypeopleaction.com for resources. Write or call your senators' offices and let them know that you care about judges who will uphold the Constitution and be fair on the bench. Then, when judges are being considered by the U.S. Senate, be sure to write and call your senators about the specific confirmations that are happening.

→ **Learn about your state and local courts.** State and local courts (as opposed to federal courts, like the Supreme Court) decide a lot of issues that matter to you and your community's everyday life. In some states, you may have more rights than even the federal Constitution and laws provide. In all states and local communities, it is your state and local courts that decide issues like child custody issues, many contract disputes, landlord-tenant issues, many criminal charges, and the like.

→ **Many state and local judges are elected.** Learn about who your state and local judges are and whether they support fair and impartial interpretations of the law.

- **Your state has a state Supreme Court that interprets your state constitution and other statewide issues.** The composition of your state's Supreme Court is important, and these judges are often elected (i.e., they do not have lifetime appointments). The **National Center for State Courts** has good resources for you to learn about the judges and how you can be involved in their elections or appointments. Block time off on your calendar to explore their site (ncsc.org).

- **If you are a lawyer, support your local bar association.** If you are a lawyer, be sure you are registered and active with your local and state bar association. Follow judicial developments and know the ways you can help people access justice and the courts.

IF YOU HAVE A DAY

- **Visit your local courthouse.** Our justice system enables people to participate, so be sure to respond to jury duty summons and do your part to participate when you are called. Beyond this, understanding what happens in local courts can be a good step for some people who have an interest in local issues. Remember that hearings are open to the public, so a visit to the local courthouse can be a good way to learn more (also especially for kids). Judges face increasing violent threats. It can be supportive to meet those who work at the courthouse, including courthouse security, to thank them. If while you are at the courthouse you would like to help your immigrant neighbors, you'll find related resources at ordinarypeopleaction.com to assist you in doing so.

LONGER-TERM EFFORTS

- **Encourage lawyers whom you believe in and who reflect your community to become judges.** Lawyers of high integrity, who are fair and have a passion for law and democracy, should consider becoming a judge. Encouraging lawyers in your life to explore this pathway is one way to ensure that our courts reflect all of us.

- **Support federal court reform efforts.** The U.S. Constitution enables Congress to pass a range of reforms to ensure that federal judges operate with integrity and that the federal courts provide justice and serve as a check for the American people.

  Currently, the Supreme Court does not have an enforceable code of ethics, although legislation has been proposed to create one. Other reform proposals include consideration of term limits, changes to the Supreme Court's composition (expanding the number of judges), and expanding the number of judges in district and appeals courts to ensure there are enough judges to hear disputes. Ensure that your lawmakers know that fair courts are important to you. Start by contacting your U.S. senators and members of Congress.

- **Support organizations that work for important reforms.** A number of organizations are committed to supporting a fair judiciary and important reforms, including an enforceable code of ethics for the Supreme Court. You can learn more at ordinarypeopleaction.com.

Our Constitution is a living document that has been amended and re-amended over time. (We do, in fact, get to be in charge of what is in the Constitution!) We should not settle for a constitution that does not have an Equal Rights Amendment or one in which special interests are able to twist the existing guarantee of equal protection under the law to actually make government *less just and equitable*. As in the past, these changes—and so many others—will not come about if we, the people, don't demand and work for them.

WHAT IS THE EQUAL RIGHTS AMENDMENT?

The Equal Rights Amendment is a proposed constitutional amendment that, if formally recognized, would make sex-based equality expressly protected and spelled out in the U.S. Constitution for the first time in history. It would prohibit sex-based discrimination (including discrimination based on gender) and would enable Congress to pass legislation to address such discrimination, including in areas of workers' rights (salary, wages, pay), healthcare (including reproductive choice), education, and more. A constitutional amendment cannot be vetoed by a president. Three-fourths of U.S. states have ratified the Equal Rights Amendment. Learn more about how to support the Equal Rights Amendment (and about constitutional amendments) at ordinarypeopleaction.com.

The point here is that this moment is not just about fighting to preserve our democratic norms and systems; the point is to be honest about our past and the future we need to create for the *next* 250 years of our nation. Just as Donald Trump and Elon Musk sought to follow the motto associated with Silicon Valley (and copied by

Mark Zuckerberg) to "move fast and break things," we must now take up the mantle to move fast and fix things.[12]

What can we do to bring about a reimagined democracy? We must vote and choose leaders who will bring about real change, as we discussed in Action 1. Yet we must also play our own part in reimagining a democracy built for today and for tomorrow. If that feels big and scary, take it one step at a time. Maybe get comfortable with the actions laid out in Actions 1 through 5 first, then revisit this chapter. When you're ready, the following page features a list of steps you can take to ground yourself in the reality of the future you want to build—the change that you want to bring about in our nation.

Keeping our minds focused on the goal—a reimagined democracy that works for all of us—will help us build resilience and resolve for the fights ahead. It will also help to ensure that the sacrifices so many people are making—contending with fear while actively choosing courage—are worth it. And if nothing else, remember that our country was founded on the promises of equality and the pursuit of happiness: It is your right to dream of and work toward a future that reflects your values and the needs of your family, friends, and community. We must work to ensure that we use this current crisis as a catalyst for change that works for all of us, not just for those who have historically held the reins of power.

So, as you are taking action, be sure to remember the full picture of what you—and we, together—are fighting for. Explore the steps on the next page.

TO-DO LIST

To Rebuild Democracy, Reimagine

These are steps to keep us focused on the future we are working toward.

This can be done by yourself, with your family or loved ones, or in social groups you bring together to take action. This is also an excellent activity to do with children and young people, as they often have a clear view of what a future society should be.

Head to ordinarypeopleaction.com for inspiration or to share your stories.

- ➔ **Vent.** What are the injustices you see? What is not working in our society and in our country? Write your answers down.
- ➔ **Dream.** What is your dream for a future society? How can you transform the injustices and brokenness you see to build this future? What do you want the world to look like? Explore your ideas and write them down.
- ➔ **Collect and create.** As you reflect on the dream, collect images, art, poems, articles, memories, pictures, songs, films, books, anything that represents this dream for you. You could add some of these items to a poster board (create a vision board or dream board), or you could place these inspirational items around your home, workplace, or other spaces to remind you of the future you are seeking to build. (Near my desk, I keep a piece of artwork that my son created when he was very young—it features the word "love" and reminds me of the simple, pure values our children have and how we can create a world to reflect these values.) If you like creating art, writing, or

expressing yourself through music, consider creating your own work that reflects your dream.

- **Act.** Can you take action today to bring about the change you want to see? Perhaps there are appealing options outlined in earlier chapters, or perhaps you'll need to get creative. Be sure to also reflect on your own practices. If you want to see a world that treats all people with equal dignity, make sure you are practicing this in your everyday life. If you want to see a world where people use sustainable practices and take care of our earth and environment, model these practices in your life.

- **Support and demand.** Support candidates and elected leaders whose vision is not just to rebuild the old systems but to reimagine democracy in a way that meets the moment and future for our country. Explore ways to make demands of other institutions as well, such as large corporations or suppliers. Explore efforts like Democracy Works 250, a new initiative that is reimagining—and doing the work to realize—a democracy that works for all people for the next 250 years. You can explore this at democracyworks250.org and find more resources at ordinarypeopleaction.com.

Don't lose heart. In times when tragedy, fear, and terror are unfolding on a near-daily basis, use the dreams you have amassed above to remain optimistic. Understand and reflect on the time it takes to achieve progress and work with urgency each day to bring about the world you want to see realized.

THE TOOLS FOR THE FIGHT

A reimagined democracy is based on an honest assessment of our past—we must understand that our democracy, which is under attack today, was not perfect or complete before the most recent attacks begin. Remembering our past also means remembering the tools that helped ordinary people make real change. This includes understanding the power of direct, nonviolent collective action.

In the earlier chapters in this book, I outlined steps that you as an individual can take to help make change and foster democracy. Individual action is important, but to make system-wide changes collective action is required. That is because ordinary people do not always have the ear of the powerful or of those capable of making system-wide change. This means that people have to resort to active tactics *in addition to* voting and safeguarding elections to make change. In so many words, people-powered tools are more effective when they are combined with political power in our political system. So, it's imperative we all vote. But we can't stop there. I structured this book to help you get started with actions you can take as an individual or in a small group within your community; change must start with the individual. For meaningful, sustained change, we must collectively join together. That is what our history teaches us, and joining together is what our future requires.

Throughout history, collective action—acts that ordinary people can take together—has been a major driver of social change. Politicians are all too often followers—and even well-intentioned ones must be pushed by the people. Indeed, the late Supreme Court Justice Louis Brandeis—who, before he was appointed to the U.S. Supreme Court, was a lawyer taking on oligarchs and the powerful—would remind us, "The only title in our democracy superior to that of president is the title of citizen."[13] In Brandeis's time the tools of collective action were frequently used: mass peaceful demonstrations, strikes, and boycotts. These are the tools of the labor movement, the civil rights movement, the immigrants' rights movement, and others. And they are tools we must continue to use today.

The Tip Sheet below provides information on collective action. There are many more resources in the chapter notes at ordinarypeopleaction.com.

TIP SHEET

Nonviolent Direct Action Methods

What is collective action? Collective action is when a group of people or institutions work together to achieve a common goal, often sharing resources and tactics.

What is a strike? A strike is an organized, collective stop to one's work enacted by employees to put pressure on management to change working conditions. Strikes have been used to demand better pay, working conditions, safety standards, and more.

Work stoppages and community shutdowns. Strike-like actions aimed at the government or oppressive systems are when large portions of the labor force stop working to protest system-wide conditions (some people refer to this as a general or mass strike or a work or community shutdown). In January 2026, peaceful protesters in Minneapolis, Minnesota, closed businesses and did not go to work—in a move that the United States had not seen in eighty years—to protest the Trump-Vance administration's violence toward people and ICE raids. Local businesses closed in solidarity and everyone from students to retirees marched.

What is a boycott? Another form of collective action, a boycott is the refusal to use or buy goods or services from a particular person, company, or country to demand a change in either the way the producer or seller is operating or to bring about changes to the economy overall by putting pressure on people in power (like politicians) to change laws or conditions. Recently, civil rights organizers and faith leaders have led a boycott against Target, and consumers boycotted The Walt Disney Company (to protest the cancellation of Jimmy Kimmel's show) and Spotify (for running ICE recruitment ads). A ***blackout*** or ***system-wide boycott*** is a withdrawal of spending or buying by a substantial part of the population to pressure institutions to make changes.

What are other forms of nonviolent, direct action? Other forms of collective action include mass demonstrations and protests. In some instances, people choose to protest a law they believe to be unjust through not following the law. This is what Dr. King did when he was imprisoned in the Birmingham City Jail. It is known as peaceful civil disobedience. Other forms of lawful, nonviolent collective action include hunger strikes, prayer vigils, digital pressure campaigns, concerts and art installations, and many more.

How do I participate in collective action today? Start first by examining your position and how you can best express your values. There are a number of ways to participate in lawful, nonviolent collective action through organizing in your community, participating in nationwide boycotts, or demonstrations and protests. There will be moments when this type of collective action is required to protect our communities, our elections, and our democracy. The resources at ordinarypeopleaction.com can point you to some opportunities for action.

No Kings and Collective Action

Millions of people have taken to the streets to demand that the government be accountable and to declare "No Kings" in response to the Trump-Vance administration's extremism. The No Kings protests were one of the largest single-day demonstrations in U.S. history. Log on to nokings.org to learn how you can participate in lawful, nonviolent actions in your community. Find other resources on how to incorporate collective action into your daily life, including mobilizations important to defend voting rights, at ordinarypeopleaction.com. The site includes resources for getting your kids civically active.

ACTION 7

Keep Going: The Only Way Out Is Through

"IT DIDN'T HAPPEN OVERNIGHT." I had asked my grandmother how long it took for the Southern magnolia trees in my grandparents' small Texas town to go from bulbs to majestic blooms. "Years and years," she said, "It takes care, time, and sun." My grandparents lived in Magnolia, a small east-Texas town. The town was known for its tall pine trees, its railroad, and, yes, its magnolia trees. But when my grandmother moved to Magnolia decades before I was born, there were no magnolia trees on her farm or in her yard. So, she began planting. She planted magnolia trees on her farm, in her yard, and also in city spaces, like at the public school and town hall. By the time I was growing up, I would never have known that her farm once lacked magnolia trees amidst its already mighty pines. The glorious white blossoms and distinctive dark-green leaves are in the background of so many of my memories—and all because of my grandmother's work of planting and tending over the decades. As a child of the Great Depression, material things were not where she found her comfort. Instead, she appreciated the beauty that could emerge from planting a single bulb or seed and the years of nurturing that followed—for her it was the greatest inheritance she could leave.

I have found myself thinking of those magnolia trees often these last months as I have traveled the country and spent time with so many people experiencing despair, and as I, too, have struggled with moments of deep doubt and feelings of helplessness. Many of us find ourselves lost—afraid of where the nation is heading and desperately wanting to flip the proverbial switch but overwhelmed by the fact that there isn't just one switch to flip. There are concerns at the state and local levels. At the Supreme Court. In Congress. And, in the White House. People are angry at the daily incursions on their rights, at the layers upon layers of corruption as a president and his allies enrich themselves while millions struggle to make ends meet. They have witnessed innocent people, including American citizens, be killed at the hands of their own government. They are scared by the deportations, disappearances, and detentions. They have woken up to masked agents on the streets and community members afraid or, worse, gone. They are bewildered and enraged by overreach and lawlessness, by the blatant disregard for our rights. They are angered by the Supreme Court's decimation of voting rights, and by the historic numbers of unexplained decisions on its shadow docket that prevent people from being protected by lower court rulings by not considering the full record or hearing argument. A friend said to me, "Even when we see the wins your team achieves in court, or are inspired by millions in the streets, or are encouraged by off-cycle election victories, we wake up the next day to another nightmare. It seems as if nothing we do matters." This is an understandable and real feeling.

And it may not go away.

The feelings of hopelessness, defeat, and powerlessness are a feature, not a bug, of the political machine replacing our democracy with autocratic rule. In fact, the number one tool that autocratic leaders use to consolidate power is not voter suppression, election denialism, or gerrymandering—it is convincing people that there is nothing they can do to change their circumstances. That they have no power. Convincing people to give up. That any effort to save our nation is too late, too futile, and too naïve.

And that's why, despite these feelings, or in the face of these feelings, we must keep going.

We must commit to ourselves—and to one another—that we will not succumb to the belief that we have no power. We DO have power. And we need to find and use it.

We must also have the determination to look at where we are—at the harms and the realities and heartbreaks—and to not look away. To see it for all that it is. We are living in a nation that is rapidly backsliding into autocracy. Our institutions were not delivering for us before and now, stressed and tested to the point of collapse, they are delivering even less. We must be able to see what is happening and understand: *This is where we are. There are no shortcuts out of this. The only way out is through.*

But we are far from powerless.

We must do everything we can in our communities and in all upcoming elections to halt the backslide to autocracy. We also have to remember that the work must continue over time. Journalist and historian Anne Applebaum, who has studied rising authoritarianism across the globe, reminds us that autocratic threats "cannot easily be defeated or dismissed in one electoral cycle."[1] Just as magnolia trees can take decades to reach maturity, and need steady tending along the way, creating a society that cares for all of us needs active, ongoing efforts. There are no quick fixes to a long-term challenge.

As I have talked with people who are in despair about the seemingly impossible task we have ahead, I have turned to the words of muckraking photojournalist Jacob A. Riis, who documented the seemingly immovable abject poverty faced by people in New York City in the late 1800s as the rich lived in gilded mansions. I first discovered Riis when studying economics, learning how the inhumane conditions experienced by many at the end of the Gilded Age, documented in Riis's powerful photojournalism book *How the Other Half Lives: Studies among the Tenements of New York*, gave rise to the progressive movement in the early twentieth century. In law school, I learned that this movement had to work against every institutional power structure—including the Supreme Court—to demand real change. Riis wrote in his memoir, *The Making of An American*, "When nothing seems to help, I go and look at a stonecutter hammering away at his rock, perhaps a hundred times without as much as a crack showing in it. Yet at the hundred and first blow it will split in two, and I know it was not that blow that did it, but all that had gone before."[2]

Eventually, Riis's work helped shine an important light and contributed to a movement that brought about significant social reforms—from wage and hour laws to worker safety laws, child worker protections, and more. But the work was long and arduous. It was not solved in one election cycle or through one initiative.

The work we must do now is day-by-day, hammer-by-hammer, step-by-step work. We must do what Dr. Martin Luther King Jr., called the work to "hew out of the mountain of despair a stone of hope."[3] We must remember too, that though some may consider this a new fight, we are building on the movements and actions of people who have been hammering away at the struggle for representation, freedom, and justice for a long time—including those in the Black, Brown, Indigenous, immigrant, and LGBTQ communities. Movement builders and communities with the lived experience of persistent injustice know that the work continues beyond one election cycle.

The only way out is through. The work of justice has always been urgent. The ultimate action that strikes the blow to injustice—and, yes, to autocracy—will make its mark because of the work of ordinary people like you who in this extraordinary time took singular steps, day by day, conversation by conversation, to move the mountain of despair. The majestic magnolia blossoms started from a single bulb that did not develop and bloom until years later. The ultimate split in the rock happens after many hammers. Both recent events and our rich history teach us that what is on the other side of this crisis is, in fact, up to us. But it will take us all doing our part. There are no shortcuts. The only way out is through.

And so, we come to the final action in this book—and perhaps the most important: As ordinary people living in an extraordinary time, our task is to keep going. Every day, do the next thing. Do not let the size of our task deter you from pushing through, from taking the next step, from finding the next stone of hope and taking action.

We do this in our lives every day. We find ways of persisting through tragedy, the death of loved ones, the loss of jobs, the breaking of relationships, the betrayal of friends. We are resilient and powerful, and we must bring our strengths to the work of our communities and our nation. This is the work of our lives. It is what our children and their children will inherit.

And you are not alone. You stand alongside so many people who came before you and who are here with you now. I'm with you, as is our team at Democracy Forward, and so are countless lawyers, advocates, and policymakers who are working for positive change along with so many other concerned individuals working in their communities. You are with every other person reading this book.

To keep going, we must take care of ourselves and our communities. We must be willing to rest when we are tired, but never, ever quit. "Like a crop in the field, justice must be nurtured and grown," workers' rights advocate, organizer, and Presidential Medal of Freedom honoree, Dolores Huerta, said to me recently when we were reflecting on the long road ahead.[4] Her eyes sparkled. "They can cut all the flowers, but they can't hold back the spring," she said, paraphrasing Chilean poet Pablo Neruda as she often does. *They can't hold back the spring.*[5] In this moment, we stand on her shoulders and on the shoulders of so many others—including revolutionaries who threw off the reins of monarchy, enslaved people who stood up to unspeakable violence and degradation, abolitionists who defeated the centuries-old institution of human slavery, the suffragists and freedom fighters in World War II, the freedom riders of the civil rights movement, workers' rights organizers, and the resisters of our time.

But change will not come about if we don't pick up our shovels and get to work today. We must meet the urgency of this moment and also accept the long road ahead. We can take pride in the fact that democracy has always been the underdog and that the democracy we seek to build—one in which all are served—has not yet existed. If where we are right now seems hard and overwhelming, that's because it is. You exist in a moment that future generations will look on as extraordinary—a moment in which it is you who needs to bring about change. We all have a role to play.

What Roosevelt said all those years ago to another generation of Americans living in an extraordinary time applies to our own: "This generation has a rendezvous with destiny."[6] Dismiss the nagging feeling that your voice doesn't matter, that you have no power, and that we, together, cannot overcome. Nix the cynicism—all too often it is the language of the elite who feel they've gamed it all out, declared a situation hopeless, and retreated. World-changing movements for freedom never start with the powerful but always with the people. We all, each of us, need to be part of this movement in this extraordinary time.

When you are tired or overwhelmed, rest and restore yourself, but do not quit. Keep your shovel near; and then, when you are restored, pick it up. In small ways that will add up and become big, hold your community, extend your circle, protect your neighbor, face your fear. Find your courage, embrace joy, and remember our history. Now, pick up your shovel. The seeds you plant and tend to will bloom with time. ***Keep going. Just keep going.***

Put on Your Cape and Reclaim Your Power

- **Pick up a shovel.** Focus on what you can do and try to confront what you find overwhelming in the world. Remember that your decisions and actions matter. If you find yourself spiraling, work through the mindset shift presented in Action 1 and also remember the rituals for finding elements of joy in Action 6.

- **Achieve information sobriety.** Be intentional about your media consumption. Do not let the media lead you down a spiral; be careful about when and how you consume it. Check to make sure information is factual. Develop media habits that are healthy for you and your life. Support local and nonprofit media as well as new media sources, including creators who are accurately reporting and building trust.

- **Start at your front door.** Democracy is not an abstraction; it begins at your front door. Even if the first step is just getting to know your neighbors, take it; engage, then expand from there. Our connections to our communities are critical at a time when polarizing actors seek to build divisions between people. This is a dark and scary time; be prepared to protect yourself, family, and neighbors. Know your rights.

- **Practice tailgate accountability.** Lean into opportunities and spaces to get to know people with different backgrounds and beliefs. Build connection and deconstruct the caricatures people may have of you (and be open to adjust your impressions of them). We will all be richer in our experiences for knowing and building community with people who are not like us. Don't let the intimacy of a space or relationship put you in a situation where you are complicit in fostering fear and hatred toward other people and groups; be accountable here too.

- ➔ **Get serious about fear, courage, and joy.** Don't let fear write the last chapter of your or our nation's story. Be curious about your fear and take the steps to choose courage. Don't underestimate joy—embrace your joy and build rituals that replenish and fuel you.

- ➔ **Remember the past, fight for the future.** Don't let the odds deter you; throughout our nation's history, other people have overcome dark times. At the same time, understand that rebuilding democracy requires reimagining systems and structures that can hold all of us. Be part of the generational work of demanding more and creating a nation that truly serves all of us and affirms everyone's equal dignity. Use the tools that have been tried and true in the past—above all, nonviolent direct collective action—to fight for the future.

- ➔ **Keep going.** Do not be discouraged. Rest when you need to. Then dive into the rituals that bring you joy and renew your spirit. We have a long journey ahead. We are planting the seeds of the future. The only way out is through, but if we move together—with our values intact and courage in our hearts—as ordinary people, we can meet what this extraordinary time requires of us.

Never, ever, give up.

Visit ordinarypeopleaction.com for more tools for the journey ahead.

Silence in the face of authoritarianism is complicity. Speaking out is a patriotic act. Democracy doesn't defend itself. It requires participation, vigilance, and courage from ordinary people.[1]

–*Rob Reiner*

We know that democracy does not mean the coercion of all into a deadly—and, finally, wicked—mediocrity but the liberty for all to aspire to the best that is in him, or that has ever been.[2]

–*James Baldwin*

Acknowledgments

WRITING THIS BOOK WOULD NOT have been possible without the generosity, brilliance, and dedication of so many people.

To the people of this nation who have stepped forward in this time—whether through community action, public service, rendering mutual aid, building stronger bonds, raising kind children, becoming more informed, having hard conversations, going to court, voting, volunteering, speaking out, changing your minds, engaging with this book, helping a friend in need, or being catalysts for courage—thank you. You are the reason for this book, and you will make the change needed in our nation.

To people across the world who are opposing autocracy and working to strengthen or bring about democracy in your own nations—from Ukraine to Brazil, to Hungary to Nepal, and everywhere in between—thank you for showing us what it means to fight for freedom.

To every single member of the team at Democracy Forward, our unparalleled supporters, our dedicated partners, loyal board members, incredible alumni, and, most important, the communities we are honored to represent and serve: This book would not have been possible without you. Thank you.

To Thea, Kate, Josie, Chloe, Allison, and the entire Ten Speed Press team, thank you for believing in this project during such a critical time and for your support in bringing it to fruition.

To Meg of Thompson Literary, thank you for approaching me about writing this book and for your guidance, your advocacy, and your support.

The list of people who contributed to, inspired, read early drafts, and informed this book could fill a volume of its own. You know who you are. Thank you from the bottom of my heart.

To the artists, musicians, dancers, creators, actors, comedians, writers, poets, and journalists, thank you for continuing to create, investigate, and inspire even when the world is at a breaking point.

To every teacher and mentor who was generous enough to help me learn, improve, and find my voice, thank you. A special thank-you to the public-school educators who mentored me in K-12 and to the incredible faculty at my alma maters: Baylor University and the Georgetown University Law Center.

To the two firms where I began my legal career: Covington & Burling LLP and WilmerHale, thank you for teaching me how to be a lawyer. And thank you for not capitulating to the unconstitutional demands and threats the administration has made against you for representing your clients, upholding the rule of law, and being true to our code of professional ethics as lawyers.

To my family and friends, your steadfast support means more than I can say. I am deeply, endlessly grateful.

To Lucy, Roman, Ferris, and Biza Skye, you were the first children I loved as my own, and you have always inspired me to look toward the future.

To Cole and Renick, you are my joy, my motivation, and my greatest loves. Thank you for everything.

And to those no longer here but who came before us and showed us how to live in disappointment and to overcome insurmountable odds to win our freedom and the freedom of our neighbors, may you see our gratitude in the actions we take to meet our generation's own moment.

Notes

OPENING EPIGRAPHS

1. Frederick Douglass, "Frederick Douglass Declares There Is No Progress Without Struggle," *SHEC: Resources for Teachers,* accessed February 23, 2026, shec.ashp.cuny.edu/items/show/1245.
2. Franklin D. Roosevelt, "Acceptance Speech for the Renomination for the Presidency, Philadelphia, Pa.," *The American Presidency Project*, June 27, 1936, presidency.ucsb.edu/documents/acceptance-speech-for-the-renomination-for-the-presidency-philadelphia-pa.
3. Barbara Jordan,"1976 Democratic National Convention Keynote Address," *American Rhetoric,* July 12, 1976.

"FORWARD"

1. "Read Conservative Judge's Full Opinion Rebuking Trump Administration over Abrego Garcia Case," *Time*, April 17, 2025, time.com/7278774/judge-harvie-wilkinson-opinion-read-full-text-trump-abrego-garcia/.
2. Ivan Pereira, "Trump Reacts to Joe Rogan's Warning About Becoming 'Monsters' over Deportations, No Due Process," ABCNews.com, April 30, 2025, abcnews.com/Politics/trump-reacts-joe-rogans-warning-becoming-monsters-deportations/story?id=121284580. Accessed March 2, 2026.
3. Roosevelt, "Acceptance Speech."

ACTION 1

1. Benedict Vigers and Julie Ray, "Record Numbers of Younger Women Want to Leave the U.S.," Gallup, November 13, 2025, news.gallup.com/poll/697382/record-numbers-younger-women-leave.aspx.

2. John Stuart Mill, "On Liberty" (Dover Publications, June 19, 2002). Original work published 1859.
3. Erwin Chemerinsky and Michael Luttig, "A Refresher Course in American Truths," *Los Angeles Times,* Voices, July 4, 2025, latimes.com/opinion/story/2025-07-04/united-states-democracy-principles-july-4. These principles undergird an initiative, We Hold These Truths, where Americans of different political and ideological backgrounds are committing to these essential elements of our democratic republic. More information is available at weholdtruths.org.
4. The International Institute for Democracy and Electoral Assistance, "Global State of Democracy Report 2021: Building Resilience in a Pandemic Era," *IDEA Global Report* (2021), idea.int/gsod-2021/global-report/.
5. *IDEA,* "Global State" (2021).
6. *IDEA,* "Global State" (2021).
7. "Statement of Concern: The Threats to American Democracy and the Need for National Voting and Election Administration Standards," *New America,* June 1, 2021, newamerica.org/political-reform/statements/statement-of-concern/.
8. "13 Presidential Libraries from Hoover to Obama Warn of Fragile State of U.S. Democracy," *PBS News,* September 7, 2023, pbs.org/newshour/politics/13-presidential-libraries-from-hoover-to-obama-warn-of-fragile-state-of-u-s-democracy. Accessed February 25, 2026.
9. David Pilgrim, "What Was Jim Crow," Jim Crow Museum, Ferris State University, September 2000 (edited in 2012), jimcrowmuseum.ferris.edu/what.htm.
10. *Shelby County v. Holder,* 570 U.S. 529 (2013).
11. Jesse Colombo, "America's Wealth Inequality Is at Roaring Twenties Levels," *Forbes,* February 28, 2019, forbes.com/sites/jessecolombo/2019/02/28/americas-wealth-inequality-is-at-roaring-twenties-levels/.
12. Sarah Steimer, "Income Inequality Has Led to an Erosion of Democracy in Countries Around the World," The University of Chicago, Department of Political Science, January 7, 2025, socialsciences.uchicago.edu/news/income-inequality-has-led-erosion-democracy-countries-around-world.
13. "Home—the Stakes Are Too High: Voting, Civic Engagement and Political Participation," University of Delaware, 2024, exhibitions.lib.udel.edu/the-stakes-are-too-high/home/. Accessed March 30, 2026.
14. Theodore Roosevelt, "Citizenship in a Republic."
15. Jordan,"1976 Keynote Address."
16. "Tressie McMillan Cottom Joins Geoff Bennett for Our 'Settle In' Podcast," *PBS News,* January 26, 2026, pbs.org/newshour/show/tressie-mcmillan-cottom-joins-geoff-bennett-for-our-settle-in-podcast.
17. "Tressie McMillan Cottom," *PBS News.*

ACTION 2

1. Kirsten Eddy and Elisa Shearer, "How Americans' Trust in Information from News Organizations and Social Media Sites has Changed Over Time," Pew Research Center, October 29, 2025, pewresearch.org/short-reads/2025/10/29/how-americans-trust-in-information-from-news-organizations-and-social-media-sites-has-changed-over-time/.
2. "The Weather Channel Named #1 Most Trusted News Source Once Again," The Weather Company, May 31, 2024, weathercompany.com/news/the-weather-channel-named-1-most-trusted-news-source-once-again/.
3. Eddy and Shearer, Pew Research Center, October 29, 2025.
4. Joseph Lichterman, "Americans Don't Have Much Trust in Social Media as a Source of News, a New Report Says," Nieman Lab, April 18, 2016, niemanlab.org/2016/04/americans-dont-have-much-trust-in-social-media-as-a-source-of-news-a-new-report-says/.
5. Stacy Schiff, *The Revolutionary: Samuel Adams* (Little, Brown and Company, 2022).
6. Justin Spike, "How Hungary's Orbán Uses Control of the Media to Escape Scrutiny and Keep the Public in the Dark," Associated Press, July 31, 2024, ap.org/news-highlights/spotlights/2024/how-hungarys-orban-uses-control-of-the-media-to-escape-scrutiny-and-keep-the-public-in-the-dark/.
7. Ashley Lutz, "These 6 Corporations Control 90% of the Media in America," *Business Insider,* June 14, 2012, businessinsider.com/these-6-corporations-control-90-of-the-media-in-america-2012-6.
8. Ben H. Bagdikian, *The New Media Monopoly: A Completely Revised and Updated Edition With Seven New Chapters* (Beacon Press, 2004).
9. Betsy Woodruff Swan and Kyle Cheney, "Trump Expressed Support for Hanging Pence during Capitol Riot, Jan. 6 Panel Told," *Politico,* May 25, 2022, politico.com/news/2022/05/25/trump-expressed-support-hanging-pence-capitol-riot-jan-6-00035117; Ashley Murray, "Trump Threatens Democratic Lawmakers Including Slotkin, Calling Remarks 'Seditious' on Truth Social," *Michigan Advance,* November 20, 2025, michiganadvance.com/2025/11/20/trump-threatens-democratic-lawmakers-including-slotkin-calling-remarks-seditious-on-truth-social/.
10. Office of the Surgeon General, "Social Media and Youth Mental Health: The U.S. Surgeon General's Advisory," U.S. Department of Health and Human Services, 2023, hhs.gov/surgeongeneral/reports-and-publications/youth-mental-health/social-media/index.html.

ACTION 3

1. Ray Bradbury, *Fahrenheit 451* (Del Rey Books, 1992).
2. Martin Pengelly, "Criminal Liability for Librarians: The Fight against US Rightwing Book Bans," *The Guardian,* August 5, 2023, theguardian.com/books/2023/aug/05/criminal-liability-librarians-us-rightwing-book-bans-arkansas-democracy-forward.
3. Alexis de Tocqueville, *Democracy in America,* translated by Henry Reeve (London: Saunders and Otley, 1835–1840).
4. Danica Dillion et al., "National Politics Ignites More Talk of Morality and Power than Local Politics," *PNAS Nexus, NIH National Library of Medicine,* September 17, 2021, pubmed.ncbi.nlm.nih.gov/39290438/.
5. Jeffrey M. Jones, "Americans Trust Local Government Most, Congress Least." Gallup, October 13, 2023, news.gallup.com/poll/512651/americans-trust-local-government-congress-least.aspx; *see also* Jenn Hatfield, "On Issue after Issue, Americans Say Things Are Going Better Locally than Nationally," Pew Research Center, February 10, 2025, pewresearch.org/short-reads/2025/02/10/on-issue-after-issue-americans-say-things-are-going-better-locally-than-nationally/.
6. Owusu Enchoka, "Impact of Political Participation on Civic Engagement in Local Communities," *European Journal of Sociology, AJPO,* vol. 7(2; 2024), 11–22; *see also* Randolph C. H. Chan and Winnie W. S. Mak, "Empowerment for Civic Engagement and Well-Being in Emerging Adulthood: Evidence from Cross-Regional and Cross-Lagged Analyses," *Social Science & Medicine, NIH National Library of Medicine,* vol. 244 (2020), 112703; Hatfield, "On Issue after Issue."
7. "How to Promote Citizen Engagement and Participation," *National League of Cities,* September 12, 2022, nlc.org/article/2022/09/12/how-to-promote-citizen-engagement-and-participation/. Accessed February 23, 2026. "Citizen Engagement," *World Bank; see also* Chan and Mak, "Empowerment for Civic Engagement."
8. "Local Government Navigates Negative Impact of Political Polarization Better than Federal Government according to New CivicPulse/Carnegie Survey," Carnegie Corporation of New York, October 23, 2024, carnegie.org/news/articles/local-government-navigates-negative-impact-of-political-polarization-better-than-federal-government-according-to-new-civicpulsecarnegie-survey/.
9. "Local Government Navigates," Carnegie; see also "Ideological Balance Among Local Government Boards," *CivicPulse,* June 30, 2025, civicpulse.org/post/ideological-balance-among-local-government-boards. Accessed February 23, 2026.
10. Nora Delaney, "Social Capital: Predicting an Epidemic of Loneliness—and Prescribing the Solution," Harvard Kennedy School, Fall 2025, hks.harvard

.edu/faculty-research/policy-topics/social-policy/social-capital-predicting-epidemic-loneliness-and.

11. Robert Putnam, *Bowling Alone* (Simon & Schuster, 2001).
12. Evan T. R. Rosenman, "Robert Putnam Leads Keynote Discussion," *The Harvard Crimson,* February 25, 2026, thecrimson.com/article/2010/2/25/putnam-health-harvard-mental/. Accessed February 23, 2026; *see also* Jialu Streeter et al., "Sightlines Project Social Engagement: Special Report," Stanford Center on Longevity, longevity.stanford.edu/sightlines-project-social-engagement-special-report/.
13. Daniel Cox and Sam Pressler, "Disconnected: The Growing Class Divide in American Civic Life," The Survey Center on American Life, August 29, 2024, americansurveycenter.org/research/disconnected-places-and-spaces/.
14. Felicia Sullivan and Kei Kawashima-Ginsberg, "Study: 60 Percent of Rural Millennials Lack Access to a Political Life," *The Conversation,* theconversation.com/study-60-percent-of-rural-millennials-lack-access-to-a-political-life-74513.
15. Theda Skocpol, *Diminished Democracy: From Membership to Management in American Civic Life* (University of Oklahoma Press, 2003).
16. Josh Levy and Julie Miller, " 'A Republic If You Can Keep It' ": Elizabeth Willing Powel, Benjamin Franklin, and the James McHenry Journal," *Unfolding History: Manuscripts at the Library of Congress,* Blogs.loc.gov, January 6, 2022, blogs.loc.gov/manuscripts/2022/01/a-republic-if-you-can-keep-it-elizabeth-willing-powel-benjamin-franklin-and-the-james-mchenry-journal/.

ACTION 4

1. James L. Perry, "Trump's Moves to Strip Employment Protections from Federal Workers Threaten to Make Government Function Worse—Not Better," *The Conversation,* February 21, 2025, theconversation.com/trumps-moves-to-strip-employment-protections-from-federal-workers-threaten-to-make-government-function-worse-not-better-248086.
2. Diane Stirling, "The 'Great Divide': Understanding U.S. Political Polarization," *Syracuse University Today,* October 23, 2025, news.syr.edu/2025/10/23/the-great-divide-understanding-us-political-polarization/.
3. "Republicans and Democrats Increasingly Critical of People in the Opposing Party," Pew Research Center—U.S. Politics & Policy, August 9, 2022, www.pewresearch.org/politics/2022/08/09/republicans-and-democrats-increasingly-critical-of-people-in-the-opposing-party/.
4. 116th Congress, "Senate Intel Committee Releases Bipartisan Report on Russia's Use of Social Media," U.S. Senate Select Committee on Intelligence, October 8, 2019, https://www.intelligence.senate.gov/2019/10/08/press-senate

-intel-committee-releases-bipartisan-report-russia-e2-80-99s-use-social-media/.

5. Clara Ence, "2024 Election Ads on Immigration Mislead Voters," *The Washington Post,* August 18, 2024, www.washingtonpost.com/elections/interactive/2024/republican-campaign-ads-immigration-border-security/; *see also* Zane McNeill, "Republicans Spent Nearly $215M on TV Ads Attacking Trans Rights This Election," *Truthout,* November 5, 2024, truthout.org/articles/republicans-spent-nearly-215m-on-tv-ads-attacking-trans-rights-this-election/.
6. Eleanor Klibanoff, "Anti-Trans Ads Fired up Texas Republicans," *The Texas Tribune,* November 8, 2024, texastribune.org/2024/11/08/transgender-ads-motivate-texas-republicans/.
7. Rachel Kleinfeld, "Polarization, Democracy, and Political Violence in the United States: What the Research Says," Carnegie Endowment for International Peace, September 5, 2023, carnegieendowment.org/russia-eurasia/research/2023/09/polarization-democracy-and-political-violence-in-the-united-states-what-the-research-says.
8. Faith Wardwell, "Poll: Project 2025 Is Broadly Known and Severely Unpopular with Voters." *NBC News,* September 25, 2024, nbcnews.com/politics/2024-election/poll-project-2025-broadly-known-severely-unpopular-voters-rcna172660.
9. "Trump Has Rolled Out Many of the Project 2025 Policies He Once Claimed Ignorance About," NPR, January 19, 2026, npr.org/2026/01/19/nx-s1-5640006/trump-has-rolled-out-many-of-the-project-2025-policies-he-once-claimed-ignorance-about.
10. Alan Kronenberg. "How Many People Didn't Vote in the 2024 Election?" *US News & World Report,* November 15, 2024, usnews.com/news/national-news/articles/2024-11-15/how-many-people-didnt-vote-in-the-2024-election.
11. Jeffrey M. Jones and Ellyn Maese, "Americans Show Consensus on Many Democracy-Related Matters," Gallup, November 20, 2025, news.gallup.com/poll/696494/americans-show-consensus-democracy-related-matters.aspx.
12. Bryan Stevenson, *Just Mercy: A Story of Justice and Redemption* (One World, 2014).
13. Michael Nicholas Stagnaro and Eran Amsalem, "*Factual Knowledge can Reduce Attitude Polarization*," *Nature Communications,* April 23, 2025, nature.com/articles/s41467-025-58697-3.
14. David DuPont, "In BGSU Beyond the Dream Address, Eddie Glaude Jr. Sheds Light on the Darkness of the American Soul," *BG Independent News,* Bowling Green State University, January 21, 2023, bgindependentmedia.org/in-bgsu-beyond-the-dream-address-eddie-glaude-jr-sheds-light-on-the-darkness-of-the-american-soul/. Accessed February 23, 2026.

15. DuPont, "In BGSU Beyond the Dream," 2023.
16. Jordan, "1976 Keynote Address."
17. News, "WATCH: House Democrats Hold Special Jan. 6th Hearing on Five-Year Anniversary," *PBS News,* January 6, 2026, pbs.org/newshour/politics/watch-live-house-democrats-hold-special-jan-6th-hearing-on-five-year-anniversary. Accessed February 23, 2026.

ACTION 5

1. Geoff Duncan, "January 6: Five Years Later, Opening Statement," House Committee on the Judiciary, January 6, 2026, democrats-judiciary.house.gov/sites/evo-subsites/democrats-judiciary.house.gov/files/evo-media-document/panel-3-duncan-opening.pdf.
2. Scott Pelley et al., "Fired Justice Department Lawyer Says He Refused to Lie in the Abrego Garcia Case," *CBS News,* October 19, 2025, cbsnews.com/news/erez-reuveni-justice-department-whistleblower-kilmar-abrego-garcia-60-minutes/. Accessed 20 October 2025.
3. Robert J. Taylor et al., eds., *Papers of John Adams, Volumes 3 and 4: May 1775–August 1776* (Harvard University Press, 1979), 86–93.
4. Samuel Rosenman, ed., *The Public Papers of Franklin D. Roosevelt, Volume Two: The Year of Crisis, 1933* (University of Michigan Library, 2005), 11–16.
5. "Trump Supporters Are More Likely to Expect Collapse into Fascism," *The Washington Post,* October 23, 2024, washingtonpost.com/politics/2024/10/23/trump-supporters-are-more-likely-expect-collapse-into-fascism/.
6. Erin Mulvaney et al., "The Law Firms That Appeased Trump—and Angered Their Clients," *The Wall Street Journal,* June 1, 2025, wsj.com/us-news/law/law-firms-trump-deals-clients-71b3616d?gaa_at=eafs&gaa_n=AWEtsqeOS3GyHyl5DKlRoDQUMSp_-gtfIzK7ctdjZBy6h_Gsvwm9PM45bd-zaKs_a50%3D&gaa_ts=699f00bd&gaa_sig=ogwJUH82gBpbY5emQxnY8Yre5ytOhlOuZU_9l3yaYoaL2mi7aKCDm5Aq_F9atnDNWXwwXgKH2VohF4Z_admOA%3D%3D. Accessed February 25, 2026.
7. Thomas B. Edsall, "This Is What You Get When Fear Mixes With Money," *The New York Times,* April 10, 2024, nytimes.com/2024/04/10/opinion/trump-donors-project-2025.html?unlocked_article_code=1.jU0.T48U.XULEfvvhlOeN&smid=nytcore-ios-share&referringSource=articleShare&ugrp=u&sgrp=c-cb.
8. Milton Mayer, *They Thought They Were Free: The Germans* (University of Chicago Press, 1966).
9. Theodore Roosevelt, "Citizenship in a Republic," speech at the Sorbonne, Paris, April 23, 1910, theodorerooseveltcenter.org/encyclopedia/culture-and-society/man-in-the-arena/.

10. JB Pritzker, "'What Comes Next?': Illinois Governor Delivers Stern Message on State of Country," *NBC Chicago,* February 19, 2025, nbcchicago.com/news/local/chicago-politics/what-comes-next-illinois-governor-delivers-stern-message-on-state-of-country/3678083/. Accessed February 23, 2026.
11. "CIA Honors Underground Railroad and Civil War Hero Harriet Tubman as a Model Spy with a New Statue," *NBC News,* October 1, 2022, nbcnews.com/politics/national-security/cia-honors-underground-railroad-hero-harriet-tubman-model-spy-new-stat-rcna50159.
12. Frederick Douglass, "West India Emancipation, *Two Speeches by Frederick Douglass* (C.P. Dewey, 1857), libraryweb.org/~digitized/books/Two_Speeches_by_Frederick_Douglass.pdf.
13. "Martin Luther King, Jr. Was Arrested 29 Times for Committing These 'Crimes,'" *Black History,* blackhistory.com/2019/11/martin-luther-king-jr-was-arrested-29-times-crimes.html.
14. Martin Luther King Jr., "Letter from Birmingham Jail," *Why We Can't Wait* (Harper & Row, 1964), 77–100.
15. *Dobbs v. Jackson Women's Health Organization,* 597 U.S. 215 (2022) (overturning *Roe v. Wade*); *see also* Pew Research Center, "Majority of Public Disapproves of Supreme Court's Decision to Overturn *Roe v. Wade,*" Pew Research Center, July 6, 2022, pewresearch.org/politics/2022/07/06/majority-of-public-disapproves-of-supreme-courts-decision-to-overturn-roe-v-wade/; "Support Rises for Abortion Rights after High Court Ruling," Dartmouth University, November 27, 2023, home.dartmouth.edu/news/2023/11/support-rises-abortion-rights-after-high-court-ruling. Accessed March 30, 2026; "'I Underestimated the Depth of Outrage': A Year in Post-Roe America," *Politico,* June 23, 2023, www.politico.com/news/magazine/2023/06/23/dobbs-roe-abortion-surprises-00103084.
16. Brett Beasley, "Breaking Conformity: The Power of One Lone Voice," Notre Dame Deloitte Center for Ethical Leadership, ethicalleadership.nd.edu/thought-leadership/the-power-of-one-how-a-lone-dissenter-really-can-make-a-difference.
17. Jack Gilbert, "A Brief for the Defense," *Refusing Heaven: Poems* (Alfred A. Knopf, 2005).
18. Hannah Arendt, "Amor Mundi 11/15/15," Bard College, 2025, hac.bard.edu/amor-mundi/amor-mundi-111515-2015-11-15. Accessed March 30, 2026.
19. John Swift, "Siege of Sarajevo," *Britannica.com,* July 5, 2022, britannica.com/event/Siege-of-Sarajevo.
20. Elizabeth Mehren, "And the Quartet Played On," *The Immigrant Story,* November 7, 2020, theimmigrantstory.org/and-the-quartet-played-on/.
21. Adrien Fillon, "'Culture Saved Us': In Besieged Sarajevo, Art as Resistance," *Balkan Transitional Justice,* April 4, 2025, balkaninsight.com/2025/04/04/culture-saved-us-in-besieged-sarajevo-art-as-resistance/.

22. Stonewall National Monument Visitor Center, stonewallvisitorcenter.org/about/.
23. Jane Hirshfield, "The Weighing," *The October Palace* (HarperCollins, 1994).

ACTION 6

1. "The Trump Administration Considering an Appeal on Payout of SNAP," *All In with Chris Hayes,* MS NOW, October 31, 2025.
2. David F. Levi et al., "Losing Faith: Why Public Trust in the Judiciary Matters," *Judicature,* September 10, 2022, judicature.duke.edu/articles/losing-faith-why-public-trust-in-the-judiciary-matters/.
3. "JCN Launches 'Let the People Decide' Campaign," JCN, https://judicialnetwork.com/jcn-statement/let-the-people-decide-statement/; "Conservative Group to Launch $2 million Ad Campaign to Block Supreme Court Nomination," *The Washington Post,* March 18, 2016, https://www.washingtonpost.com/news/powerpost/wp/2016/03/18/conservative-group-to-launch-2-million-ad-campaign-to-block-supreme-court-nomination/.
4. Adam Liptak, "A Supreme Court in Disarray after an Extraordinary Breach," *The New York Times,* May 3, 2022, nytimes.com/2022/05/03/us/politics/supreme-court-leak-roe-v-wade-abortion.html.
5. Nicole LaFond, "Where Things Stand: Alito's *Roe* Opinion Was Filled with Language Pushed by Evangelical Group," *Talking Points Memo,* July 25, 2022, talkingpointsmemo.com/edblog/alitos-roe-opinion-language-evangelical-group. Accessed March 30, 2026; *see also* Kara Dickinson, Tim Voght, et al., "SCOTUS Justices 'Prayed with' Her—Then Cited Her Bosses to End Roe," *Rolling Stone,* July 6, 2022, rollingstone.com/politics/politics-features/roe-supreme-court-justices-1378046/.
6. In *Trump v. Wilcox* (145 S.Ct. 1415 [2025]).
7. Erwin Chemerinsky, "Why the Shadow Docket Should Concern Us All," *SCOTUSblog,* August 4, 2025, scotusblog.com/2025/08/why-the-shadow-docket-should-concern-us-all/.
8. "The Federal Court Snapback: The Judiciary, Including the Supreme Court, Is Standing up to the President," *SCOTUSblog,* February 10, 2026, scotusblog.com/interim-docket-blog/the-federal-court-snapback-the-judiciary-including-the-supreme-court-is-standing-up-to-the-president/.
9. Barbara Jordan, "Statement on the Articles of Impeachment," speech before the House Judiciary Committee, Washington, D.C., July 25, 1974, americanrhetoric.com/speeches/PDFFiles/Barbara%20Jordan%20-%20Statement%20on%20Impeachment%20Articles.pdf.
10. Jordan, "Articles of Impeachment."
11. In *Trump v. CASA, Inc.,* 606 U.S. 381 (2025).

12. Jordan Liles, "Did Mark Zuckerberg Say, 'Move Fast and Break Things'?" *Snopes,* July 29, 2022, snopes.com/fact-check/move-fast-break-things-facebook-motto/.
13. "We the People: Resource Center: Lesson 33," Center for Civic Education, 2026, civiced.org/resourcecenter/level3/unit6/lesson33. Accessed February 23, 2026.

ACTION 7

1. Anne Applebaum, "Every Election is Now Existential," *The Atlantic,* June 6, 2025, theatlantic.com/ideas/archive/2025/06/existential-election-poland-nationalism/683051/. Accessed February 23, 2026.
2. Jacob A. Riis, *The Making of an American* (The Macmillan Company, 1901).
3. Martin Luther King Jr., "I Have a Dream," speech at March on Washington for Jobs and Freedom, August 28, 1963, Lincoln Memorial, Washington D.C., npr.org/2010/01/18/122701268/i-have-a-dream-speech-in-its-entirety.
4. These remarks were made at the Feminist Majority Foundation's 17th annual Global Women's Rights Awards and Gala in November 2025, where I was also honored.
5. Dolores Huerta, "Sí, Se Puede: Dolores Huerta on Organizing, Voting, and Building Power," *SEIU2015,* October 13, 2025, seiu2015.org/podcast/si-se-puede-dolores-huerta-on-organizing-voting-and-building-power/. Accessed February 23, 2026.
6. Franklin D. Roosevelt, "Acceptance Speech," *The American Presidency Project* (June 27, 1936).

CLOSING EPIGRAPHS

1. Greg Mitchell, "Tribute to Rob Reiner, and His Favorite Song," *Between Rock and a Hard Place,* December 15, 2025, gregmitchell.substack.com/p/tribute-to-rob-reiner-and-his-favorite. Accessed February 25, 2026.
2. James Baldwin, "An Open Letter to My Sister, Miss Angela Davis," *New York Review of Books,* January 7, 1971, nybooks.com/articles/1971/01/07/an-open-letter-to-my-sister-miss-angela-davis/.

About the Author

SKYE PERRYMAN, president and CEO of Democracy Forward and a TIME 100 honoree, is an attorney and internationally recognized leader at the forefront of advancing democracy and individual rights.

Perryman was named one of the fifty people shaping American society in 2026 by *The Washington Post* and under her leadership, Democracy Forward has been heralded as a "human rights hero" by the American Bar Association, securing major court victories that have protected due process, free speech, healthcare, education, economic opportunity, reproductive freedom, and more.

Perryman frequently appears on NBC, MS NOW, CNN, and NPR, and her work has been featured in outlets such as *The New York Times, The Washington Post, The Atlantic, Time,* and *Newsweek*. A popular speaker at venues including SXSW, Aspen Ideas, and The Texas Tribune Festival, she is recognized for blending legal expertise with accessible, inspiring storytelling.

Perryman grew up in Texas and is a proud product of K-12 public education. She holds a BA from Baylor University, a JD from Georgetown University Law Center, and is a Salzburg Global Fellow. She is mom to Renick, wife to Cole, and friend to many.